I0437679

Faith in the Eye of the Storm:
Katrina Stories in Four Voices

Belief at Work During
Natural Disasters

Janyce Jorgensen
Debra Anderson

Copyright © 2011 Janyce Jorgensen, Debra Anderson

All rights reserved.

ISBN: 1467926574
ISBN-13: 978-1467926577

Dedication

This book is dedicated to

   those who have faced the storms of life with faith and courage

   and to those who responded to the rebuilding efforts with faith and compassion

Your faith-informing-life tells a heartwarming story and gives encouragement to many

Contents

Acknowledgments vii

Initial Voices: Stories of Faith, Bindings, and Beginnings
Silence 3
Sound Bytes 4
Talk about Tomorrow 5
Sight and Sound 6
God's Original Language 7
Our Experiences 8
Our Method 12

First Voice: Stories of Faith, Courage, and Survival
"Survive" by Cee Cee Jay Spencer 19
The Best Gift, as told by Annette Richard 23
Now What?, as told by Annette Richard 43
"Secrets" by Cee Cee Jay Spencer 57
The Hardest Part, as told by Nickolas Greene 59
"Invitation" by Cee Cee Jay Spencer 69
Strength of Family, as told by Mike Kovacevich 71
Rescue, as told by Mike Kovacevich 83
Moving Forward, as told by Mike Kovacevich 101
"Beginning Again" by Cee Cee Jay Spencer 111
He's Working It Out, as told by Morris Robinson . . 113

Second Voice: Stories of Faith, Endurance, and Transformation
"Seeds of Life" by Cee Cee Jay Spencer 137
Unexpected Changes, interview with Tom Fox 141

Lost and Found, interview with Jan Freeman 149

Jill of All Trades, interview with Rava Coyle 155

Third Voice: Stories of Faith, Service and Commitment

"Clean Up" by Cee Cee Jay Spencer 169

Listening and Responding 173

Rebuilding and Building 175

Learning and Relearning 177

Giving and Receiving 179

Coming and Going (and Coming and Going) 183

Fourth Voice: Stories of Faith—Written and Unwritten, Lived Out and Hoped For

Psalm 51 191

Informing Life and Faith – Psalm 51 195

Creating 197

Renewing 199

Restoring 203

Upholding 205

The Fourth Voice 208

Lasting Voices: Stories of Faith—Past, Present, Future

Looking Back 213

Looking Forward 214

May It Be So 217

Endnotes 219

Bibliography 223

Acknowledgments

With gratitude and humility, we would like to acknowledge and thank disaster response organizations that housed and fed us along with so many other workers and volunteers. The stories of these organizations dotted the darkness of the daunting task of rebuilding with one bright spot after another: Camp Biloxi, Bethel Volunteer Ministry (including the Bethel Free Clinic), Lutheran Disaster Response,[1] and Recovery Assistance, Inc.[2]

This project would not have been possible without every storyteller who opened their hearts to share (They are identified in this story or in the endnotes).

Many others supported and helped to inform this project in various ways. We thank those along the Gulf Coast who graciously provided practical help and direction, always with a kind word. We also thank those who read this manuscript and provided helpful feedback.

With much love, we acknowledge our families. They traveled with us and without us participating in many mission trips to the Gulf Coast; they listened and encouraged us, and even lived without us during extensive travel, research, and writing. Our husbands, Richard Jorgensen and Barry Anderson, were true partners with us throughout the many years of this process.

In honor of all those who have given and still give of their time and energy, all proceeds from the sale of this book will be donated to disaster relief and recovery efforts.

We hope and pray that these pages give glory to God, the prompter, encourager, provider, and sustainer, whose gentle voice called us to this task of listening, reflecting and writing.

Initial Voices:

Stories of Faith, Bindings, and Beginnings

Silence

Silence… a paradoxical concept to begin a story, which promises to tell the faith stories born out of Hurricane Katrina in a multitude of voices. But silence, often easy to ignore, is an appropriate place in which to enter these stories of faith in the eye of the storm.

We spend our lives filling our moments of silence. When the conversation lags, we fill the silence with idle words; when the background music runs out, we look to stretch the melodies a moment longer; when the silence of anger alienates us, we seek to break through it.

Silence. Thirty hours of the sounds of the rushing waves, violent winds, and unprecedented destruction, were followed by silence. An eerie calm, a lifeless hush. In the early hours of the storm's aftermath, those who were present describe this silence in a myriad of ways: "…there were no insects or birds, no sounds of life…"; "…there was no traffic and no train…"; "…nobody could find the words in the midst of the devastation…"; "…you do not realize day to day noises until they are gone…."

Throughout human history, religious, spiritual and philosophical writings have reflected the meaning of silence. St. John of the Cross wrote that "Silence is God's original language" to which Thomas Keating added, "everything else is translation." Meister Eckert reflected that "Nothing in all creation is so like God as silence." And from the ancient Chinese philosophy of the *Tao Ching* is this admonishment, "Express yourself completely, then keep quiet. Be like the forces of nature."

For thirty hours, Hurricane Katrina expressed itself completely, and then there was silence. There was nothing left to hear, and precious little to do but to remain in that silence. Spoken words would have been inadequate, human activity would have been futile against the magnitude of what had been laid lifeless within Katrina's path.

Katrina survivors waited for the silence to give way to the voices, which would sustain them in the years that would follow. The rest of the world, stunned by their second-hand experience of Katrina through the media, waited as well.

Sound Bytes

We can hear the sounds, which break out of silence better than those, which simply ring out more loudly, and above the everyday noises of our lives and world. We are more attentive when it is out of silence that we listen.

The first and most anticipated sound byte was to "get word." Homes, towns, communities—they were destroyed—but what about the people? Where are my loved ones? How did they fare? Things—even when it is everything—can be replaced, people cannot. News that loved ones had survived was the most anticipated voice to break through the silence, but such news did not come instantly or easily. For many, the storm destroyed and swept away electricity, technology, and the ability to communicate. And, since so many were affected, so many needed to be heard from and accounted for.

Hours turned to days turned to weeks for those who waited to get word. And word came—through first responder rescue and relief efforts, through survivors' undying determination, and through love that would not give up. Stories of life were heard, even amidst the stories of death. Stories of life were the first sounds of hope to break the silence.

Talk About Tomorrow

Silence and stillness, although not synonymous, are linked to one another—so are activity and sound. The desire to move out of silent stillness following Katrina was often expressed by these words: "We have to do something." First, exhausted survivors whispered them weakly, and then they were spoken and shouted with determination by many, near and far, who wanted to help. Activity and sound linked together as an unprecedented relief effort began.

But first, these determined efforts would undergo a reality check. Gulf Coast dwellers, who had lived through or heard of prior hurricanes ("We made it through Hurricane Camille"), came to the realization that Katrina could not and would not be compared evenly to other storms. Local and federal government, in spite of its proud posture, would need to admit that the government structure was not adequately prepared for a disaster of such proportion. Well-intentioned volunteers, who trickled then flocked to the Gulf Coast to help, would need to recognize their limitations.

"We have to do something"—these words spoke of the hope for tomorrow. For Katrina survivors tomorrow would have less to do with the regular musings of tomorrow like "What are my appointments? What will I eat? What will I wear?" and more to do with coming home again. For many, tomorrow's home would be different from yesterday's home, and for too many, tomorrow would look years into the future.

Sight and Sound

Katrina survivors, first responders, volunteers, and the world would need to take a moment to see in order to believe what had happened. The visual images of the storm's aftermath would evoke shock, disbelief, and life-long visual imprints upon the minds and hearts of many. "I doubt that I will ever see anything like it again," one early volunteer said. "There were little pieces of broken glass everywhere; wherever you walked, it glittered," he continued.

"There were bodies on the Veteran's Administration property," a Biloxi resident laments, "and there were doorknobs all over the ground, but to what?"

As volunteers came to the Mississippi Gulf Coast, volunteer coordinators from local churches and organizations would often urge volunteers to take a visual tour of the area before immersing themselves in the work of the relief effort. Volunteers saw for themselves the extent of the damage: crumbled bridges, a casino barge lodged into the side of a hotel, a sea of blue roof tarps. Businesses, churches, homes, entire streets and neighborhoods were leveled and devastated. Those who saw for themselves could, in informed ways, speak, act, and play a role in the rebuilding efforts.

In the midst of more damage than the eye could see or the mind could comprehend, one visual image undergirded all others. The image was phrased as a question and posed to volunteers and residents alike, "Where did you see God today?" The question does not reference or seek to explain why God would allow such a tragedy to happen, but rather invites believers who suffer personally or with others to look for God's presence and for God at work in the midst of life's most difficult circumstances.

Ultimately, these "Face of God" conversations as they became known had very little to do with the storm's visual effects but looked beyond and behind the rubble and into the lives and hearts of people who were walking together in the days of recovery. For one volunteer, the question, "Where did you see God today?" connected him with the Holy Spirit at work. "God provides abundantly; it was amazing how the volunteers kept coming to us, and how, when we needed supplies and materials, they showed up."

"I don't get these people," a resident quipped. "They kept coming to help us, and they would stay in touch. We became attached to one another."

Residents and volunteers saw the face of God in each other. Residents were touched, even overwhelmed, by the outpouring of support and love which the volunteers brought to the coast. Volunteers, likewise, were touched and overwhelmed by the graciousness, gratitude, and hospitality of Gulf Coast residents.

God's Original Language

If we concur with St. John of the Cross, Thomas Keating, and others—that silence is God's original language—we posture ourselves in such a way that we enter into the Katrina Stories with an awareness and reverence for God's silence within the words that follow. As the stories unfold, God is there. God is behind the words, within the words, and in front of the words. God is present in the stories whether or not God is specifically mentioned.

When it became evident in the aftermath of Katrina that an extensive recovery effort would be needed, it was the faith-based organizations that stepped in to further the rebuilding efforts originally set forth by first responders. Through the presence, commitment, and perseverance of volunteers, the rebuilding effort continued and was also transformed from a rebuilding effort to a healing process.

Volunteers asked questions: "How'd you make out? How did your family make out? Why didn't your people leave?" Everyone had a story—residents spoke and volunteers listened. Hammers and brushes lay silent and motionless, if only for a minute or two, so that spiritual healing could begin and continue. First-person stories would be told over and over again. Second-hand accounts would be relayed by volunteers to others.

The pages that follow are representative stories of faith in the eye of the storm. In collecting them and telling them, there has been speaking and listening. There have been hugs and tears. There have been healing hearts and eyes of hope.

"Silence is God's original language. Everything else is translation." Every word shared in the stories to follow seeks to serve as a faithful and helpful translation of God's original language. Every word desires that the healing in the midst of the rebuilding will continue.[3]

Our Experiences—Janyce Jorgensen

It was September 4, 2005, a Sunday during the church's long season of Pentecost—a time to reflect and celebrate the growth of the church through the life and witness of disciples of all ages. Recently, the designation of this time in the church year as "Ordinary Time" had been rediscovered; but on this particular day, nothing seemed to be ordinary. Six days earlier, on August 29, 2005, the nation and the whole world watched as Hurricane Katrina hit land along the United States Gulf Coast. We watched in fear for those whose life and breath resided along those shores. We watched in compassion as the damage was assessed and first-response relief efforts begun.

As we gathered for worship on that following Sunday, I could feel my own heaviness as well as the aching hearts of those who dutifully took their seats and waited to begin. I decided that my preparations for this time of worship were inadequate in light of the circumstances, and so I asked those who were assisting with the service to allow me to go "off script" and to help provide a less-structured worship experience from the heart. And so we did. In place of the sermon I had prepared, I spoke about the events of the past week and the questions so many were asking: Why did God allow this to happen? Where is God in the midst of all this suffering?

As we worshipped that day, we fell short of discovering all the answers, but felt some comfort in living together within these questions of faith. We felt confident that God was present with the suffering, and present with us. And, we began to ask the question of what we could do to help.

On that day and in the context of worship, the event of Hurricane Katrina took hold of me and took residence in my heart. I looked for ways that I could help our hurting brothers and sisters in the Gulf Coast. Within weeks of the storm, individuals and groups from our community were traveling to the hurricane-affected areas to volunteer in the clean-up and rebuilding efforts. My first trip to Biloxi, Mississippi, was in January 2006, and many trips followed.

My skills in construction are very limited; I found my gift and contribution in talking with individuals who thought about volunteering, and in organizing groups to travel to the Gulf Coast to help. I soon discovered that these experiences were as valuable for the growth in faith of the volunteers as they were to the rebuilding and recovery efforts in which they were involved. More than homes—in fact the lives of all who were involved—were being rebuilt.

I made many return trips to the Gulf Coast to serve as a volunteer because, as I have at times articulated, I leave a piece of my heart there every time I go. Having discovered this sentiment in myself and in the lives of so many others, this book project was conceived as a way to tell and to share, to live and to celebrate the faith stories of those who have been touched and shaped by Hurricane Katrina.

Our Experiences—Deb Anderson

As we watched on TV the events that unfolded during and after Hurricane Katrina, my husband and I felt compelled to do something to help. Through the efforts of our pastor and the information she provided, in conjunction with Lutheran Disaster Response, we came to Camp Biloxi for a week in June of 2006. We returned many times.

In June of 2008 we both left our paying jobs (some call it retiring) which allowed us the opportunity to spend several weeks at a time on the Gulf Coast, working to rebuild homes. My husband is a "jack-of-all" trades and an excellent troubleshooter. His skills are definitely valued.

Although I am constantly learning new construction skills, my talents lie elsewhere. I have a heart to listen to people and to hear their tales. There are so many stories! There are stories not just from the people who survived the storm and who are trying to reclaim their lives, but also from those who volunteer both short and long term, and from the staff members of recovery organizations.

One day, after a homeowner shared her experience of surviving the storm, she commented that she would like to write her story, but that she did not have the skills to do so.

Immediately, the thought popped into my mind, stated in a quiet voice not exactly my own, "You could do that for her, Deb." I have heard this voice a few times previously in my life, calling my name to some undertaking. Although I have always enjoyed writing and appreciate a good story, I have never attempted any major writing project, nor did I have an idea of how to go about such a task.

After considering the idea and praying about it, I felt God prompting me to record stories. I thought that if this was something He wanted me to do; He would show me each step of the way. If the stories were to become a book, that would happen. Best of all, I could give each storyteller the gift of their story in type. I just had to be willing to do my part.

What blessings I have received in the process! I have learned about faith and hope and endurance and patience and growth and change and humility. I have learned about the saving grace of connections between people. I have seen first-hand how God can take a horrible situation and redeem it for something amazing. I have seen faith in the eye of the storm.

Our Method

Faith in the Eye of the Storm is a unified story told from many perspectives. Initial Voices entered the story of Katrina through the sounds and sights of residents and first responders, sharing their initial impressions and reactions to what took place on August 29, 2005. The First Voice shares the stories of Katrina survivors—of their perseverance, their strength, and their faith in the midst of their most challenging circumstances. The Second Voice shares the stories of staff and long-term volunteers, whose daily work, in contrast to what it was before the storm, became characterized by their involvement in relief efforts. The Third Voice shares the stories of volunteers, who came from all over, to help and to participate during the months and years following the storm, many of whom returned on multiple occasions to continue with the work.

Each part of the story is presented in a different voice: of the survivors from a first-person perspective, of staff and long-term volunteers from a second-person perspective, and of short-term volunteers from a third-person perspective. The stories from these different perspectives resolve to give respect and full voice to those who have so graciously shared them with us.

We discovered that in asking survivors to convey their story, we needed to say little and listen much. In interviewing staff and long-term volunteers, we discovered the questions we posed were met with full and passionate responses. In hearing the stories of volunteers, we discovered common themes, which wove these stories together in meaningful ways.

The Fourth Voice situates these stories of faith within the context of the life and witness of the Church throughout the ages. Informed by the biblical witness, we will look at the themes of creating, renewing, restoring, and upholding and how those who experienced Katrina, both during the storm and in its aftermath, recognized and were strengthened by God's activity in these ways and during these circumstances. Those who told their faith stories spoke, sometimes explicitly but often implicitly, in terms of how God was working and was present with them. In drawing out these biblical themes, we recognize that, in this moment and throughout the ages, God's presence and God's help in times of trouble is the strength that sustains us.

In outlining what *Faith in the Eye of the Storm* sets out to do, it seems appropriate and even respectful to note at the onset what this treatment will not do. In our time as volunteers in the Gulf Coast, we have encountered and become familiar with the work of thousands of volunteers, in hundreds of relief organizations; some are faith-based and others secular. We have worked alongside many, and have toured the camps and ministry sites of others, learning about their work. We have been uplifted and inspired by these stories and experiences and appreciate the value of their witness, even as they are presented from a different faith perspective or non-faith perspective. We recognize that for as many stories as we have collected and reported in this volume, there are thousands of others, which have been conveyed in other formats or have yet to be conveyed.

We write about what we know and what we have experienced in tribute and respect to all those who have their own faith stories in the eye of the storm. We write about

13

what we know and what we have experienced in the hope that these life-changing stories will continue to be told and remembered.

We also acknowledge the many other circumstances in our recent history in which stories of faith have been lived out and shared in some remarkable and meaningful ways. Prior to Hurricane Katrina, the tsunami in Southeast Asia devastated the landscape and took many lives, forever changing the circumstances of those who lived in its path. As a nation, prior to Katrina, we were still remembering the events of September 11, 2001, reeling in our post 9/11 identity, even as in late August of 2005, we were preparing to remember another anniversary of that tragic day. Following Katrina were devastating floods in the Midwest and another forceful hurricane in Texas. More recently, we know of nations forever changed by earthquakes and other natural disasters.

In the composition of this book and in the subsequent reading of it, events such as these will continue to stir us, shake us, challenge us, and move us. And…God will continue to create, renew, restore and uphold us. The stories recounted in *Faith in the Eye of the Storm*, though conditioned by time, geography, and events, are timeless stories of people of faith ready and willing to receive the help of God in seemingly helpless circumstances. These Katrina stories take their place within the witness of the people of God, past, present, and future, who relied on God's strength for their own strength during life's most difficult and challenging circumstances.

Interspersed among these stories are poems from *Katrina: Poetry in Two Distinct Voices* written by Cee Cee Jay Spencer.[4] Initially, the poems were written as a path for her personal healing in the aftermath of the storm and in her own voice. However, she recognized the value in shared healing and added a second voice to hers. The poems are read from left to right with the first voice reading the left side and the second voice reading the right side. Her powerful words inspired our listening; in tribute to her courage and in gratitude for her words, we include some of her offerings in this volume.

In the pages to follow, we write about what we know in gratitude to all those who have shared with us. We write about what we know in humility in knowing that so many others have stories to share and tell. Most importantly, we write about what we know in recognizing that in these stories of faith, we see glimpses of God's glory revealed in these circumstances, even as we experience God's invitation into the fullness of God's glory yet to come.

First Voice:

Stories of Faith, Courage, and Survival

"Survive"

Whenever the question was
posed, 'how did you get out?'
the answer was

Whenever the question was
posed, 'how did you get out?'
the answer was

'I swam with the waves'

'My clothes, torn from my
body piece by piece'

It was crazy, frightening, no
thinking could or would take
place just hoping, praying to
survive

The place I call home, our
safe haven, was reduced to
roofs and supporting beams,
the written information that
recorded our lives gone,
gone, gone

Every day is now quiet

Every day is now quiet

Mothers, the stabling force
Fathers, the financial master

A miracle

Mothers, the financial master
Fathers, the stabling force

A blessing

Children needing hugs,
smiles, time to play, time to
learn, reaching out for love

Children needing hugs,
smiles, time to play, time to
learn, reaching out for love

Agencies from all over the world opened up their doors and help just started to flow

Families returning to the days of old where grandmother, grandfather, aunts, uncles, cousins and in some cases strangers, all living under one roof

News reporting, waters surging, schools closed, vacationers mandated to leave, some homeowners preparing to stay, others board up, ready to run

Katrina on her way hits landfall some workers required to stay, others allowed to go many slowly return to emptiness and others will never return

What now?

What now?

How will we make it?

How will we make it?

When will life return to normal?

When will life return to normal?

Recovery, it's the way

Recovery, it's the way

The first voices heard are of those who endured the storm and who struggled to rebuild. These are the stories of first person encounters with the forceful winds and racing waters.

Annette Richard of Bay St. Louis, Mississippi, narrates the first two stories. **The Best Gift** *describes how her family clung to their faith and survived. In the course of events, she received a glimpse of the man her son would become.* **Now What?** *deals with the struggles of recovery and God's faithful presence.*

Nickolas Greene, Annette's son, tells the **Hardest Part.** *Nick was twelve years old when Hurricane Katrina devastated his home. This story of determination describes actions from a young man's point of view and the unique way he received God's reassurance.*

Mike Kovacevich recounts the history of old Biloxi through his family tree in **Strength of Family.** *In* **Rescue,** *he describes endeavors preparing for the storm and explains how family members and neighbors found a safe haven in his home. He also was reminded of God's presence during tough moments.* **Moving Forward** *relates the monumental task of cleaning up and putting pieces back together.*

The story of Morris Robinson of Gulfport, Mississippi, **He's Working It Out,** *illustrates faith in the God of hope amid the daunting odds of restoring his family home. God provided the means over and over.*

The Best Gift
as told by Annette Richard

Dad Won't Leave

Having gone through Hurricane Camille as a child, I am always watchful for storms during the hurricane season. As soon as one hits the Gulf of Mexico, I stay up and watch. I watch the weather Channel and the local weather. To determine the height of the waves, I check the information online from the data buoys. I look anywhere for anything that will give me additional information. As Katrina approached, I discovered there were wave heights up to fifty and sixty feet!

From this, I knew we were in trouble. My husband, Cooper, and I sat down and talked. We decided that our son, Nickolas and I, would leave. Cooper had to stay somewhere in the area because he was working for the county on the beach crew and was part of the first response team. He was also concerned for his brother.

We talked to Cooper's brother who lived next door to us and who is legally blind. You can't dig a hole in the yard without telling him, or he will fall in it because he won't see it. He can see colors and shapes. If he is close enough to you, he can see who you are. Other than that, he can't see. Stubborn man that he is, he felt that if he could make it through

Hurricane Camille, he could make it through this hurricane. He was not going to leave. So, my husband decided that he would stay in his brother's home with him.

Our son Nickolas and I were still planning on leaving. We were going to go to Cooper's Uncle Cecil's in the northern part of the state to be out of harm's way. Sunday evening, the night before the storm was to hit, we began packing our bags. By the time Nickolas and I finished, the storm was a category five. Time to get moving!

However, I got a phone call from my sister that changed our minds. I could hear my sister gritting her teeth on the phone when she announced, "Mom and Dad refuse to leave."

. My parents were both in their seventies. They were both cancer patients. My mom had just finished her chemo a month before Katrina so she was in recovery mode. She was still weak as a kitten. My dad could barely walk. His spine was fused from a rare, genetic form of arthritis called ankylosing spondylitis. His spine was like a bamboo pole. He could hardly move.

Here were two people who really should have been evacuated, but they wanted to stay to see how the house held up. They said, "Well, we made it through Camille. This area did not get any water. We'll be fine! This is a strong house."

My sister repeated, still gritting her teeth, "Mom and Dad refuse to leave." She hoped that I might have some influence over them.

I said, "Okay. I'll be over there to help." I told her that Nick and I had already packed up to leave, but that we would come there instead.

She replied, "Good! I will take care of Mom. *You* take care of Dad!"

I told her that would be fine with me. Then, I said the words to my sister that I never meant to become true, but did. I said, "I'll bring Nick and he'll float in between." At the time, I meant that he could go back and forth in between my mom and dad to help my sister and me with them. I did not mean to literally "float."

My Mom and Dad's home is only about ten to fifteen miles from our home, so we were not too far. A few minutes after my sister's frantic call, Nick and I arrived at my parent's home to spend the night. There were now the five of us in my parent's home. There was my sister Pam, my son Nickolas, my parents, and myself. My younger brother, Joseph, and his wife Donna, remained in their house, which is just behind my parent's home. However, if we decided to leave, they would come with us.

The plan was that if we had time, we would each take our own vehicles and evacuate. But, we would use my car if we had to get out in a hurry, since it was the biggest. My Expedition, which could haul nine people, had a full tank of gas. We would all just pile into it and get out. That was the deal. We found out that we did *not* have time and could not get out of there in a hurry, even if we wanted to.

As we settled down for the night, I reassured Nick that we would be fine. My parent's house was strong and we would be safe. I told him that it would not be that bad.

Early Monday morning came and we were still keeping an eye on the storm. We got up between six and seven and had breakfast. Then, we all changed our clothes, which was an unusual thing for us to do.

I had on shorts, but changed into blue jeans. I rolled up my pants' legs so that they were tight, which is something that I never do. I tucked in my shirttail, whereas I usually kept it out. So, my clothes fit more like a body suit. I even put up my hair. I braided it to keep it out of my eyes. I may put my hair into a ponytail, but I do not usually braid it, especially in such tight braids.

My son was wearing tennis shoes and he kept saying, "Mom, I don't want to wear these. I don't want to wear these tennis shoes." I told him that I had some sandals he could wear. They were the Roman style sandal with Velcro, which would be light on his feet. Unknowingly to us at the time, they later acted like flippers.

My dad switched from his long jeans to swim trunks. My mom also switched from long pants to a pair of long shorts. My sister did the same thing. Unwittingly, we had put on clothes that were better for swimming, as if we were preparing to take a dip.

As we waited for the approaching storm, we thought the best place to check for rising water was the ravine that runs alongside my parents' home. Whenever we have a storm, this is where we first see water rising. We kept checking it to see if the water was coming over its banks. Every time we peeked through the blinds at the ravine, we saw no water. With Katrina, the water never did rise in the ravine. Our usual system for checking on rising water was not going to work for us this time.

When checking the ravine, we did not want to pull the blinds up to look outside. That is a big "DON'T" during a storm. If something comes through the windows, those blinds are the only thing keeping the glass from coming in and shattering on you. You are supposed to stay away from the windows. We did keep one little set of blinds open, since it was over the kitchen sink, but it gave us a very limited view.

Although we had limited vision, we could hear. What we heard was nothing but freight train. That is what a hurricane sounds like. Tornados, which hurricanes spawn, sound the same. We had heard reports that there was a fair amount of tornado activity with Katrina. In the midst of a full-blown hurricane, the way to tell that a tornado is coming is that the sound of the freight train gets louder. The intensity gets stronger. Yet, with seventy-five mile per hour winds, it is hard to hear the difference, so we ended up having to peel back the blinds and peek out a window anyway. Is it the wind, or is it a tornado coming?

A tornado was coming! We could see its path. Luckily, it lifted up into the sky as it got to the house. However, the tail end of it clipped the chimney and popped off part of it. If it had come down and hit the house fully, we would have been in trouble right then.

After watching the tornado spin off and away, we glanced to the east and saw water coming at us from that direction. It was also coming from the south, which meant it was coming from the Gulf. We had it from two sides! We were being hit with tsunami like waves that came in hard and fast from multiple directions.

Encyclopedias!

Nick's first concern was his PlayStation, which we had brought with us. It was his most valuable possession and we needed to protect it. So, I dumped clothes out of a Ziploc bag to put the PlayStation inside.

27

However, he was upset about the possibility of losing his schoolbooks, which is funny because he hates doing homework. We had the books with him because they had just started school. He was a typical twelve-year-old boy. He was a happy-go-lucky kid overall.

For example, every year at Christmas since Nick was in pre-kindergarten, his class would do little skits. Nick was always dressed up in the Santa Claus outfit. His teacher would stuff him with a pillow. He could do a perfect "ho-ho-ho." That character really does fit his personality. His name fit, too.

After his Play Station was secure, I had to hurry up and help put up the old encyclopedias for mom. These encyclopedias have their own history, and they provided my family with a great lesson when we were younger.

During Hurricane Camille in August of 1969, we had water in our home, but it was not nearly as much as with Hurricane Katrina. It was only between two and eight inches, depending on what room you were in, as we lived in a multi-leveled home.

At the time, my parents aspired for all of us to become president of the United States, like every other good Catholic family since President Kennedy. To help us reach our potential, my parents bought a full set of Britannica encyclopedias from a traveling door-to-door salesman just before Hurricane Camille hit. They spent a fortune they did not have.

When water from Camille started coming in, the first thing my mother did was to holler, "The encyclopedias! The encyclopedias!" We had to put them all up high, out of the reach of any incoming water. She did not care about anything else. We had to save the encyclopedia set.

After they were secure, we waited. As the water started to come in, we noticed flip-flops, exiting each of our rooms. They lined up in order: my dad, my mom, my older sister, my older brother, mine, my younger brother. They lined up in order of size, one flip-flop each, all in a row, circling around in a little whirlpool, like little ducks in a row.

We started cracking up, laughing! We knew we were going to be okay. We learned that God has a sense of humor. Lighten up. Chill out. Everything is going to be okay. He reminds us of little things. His message is, "Hey, joke, laugh, lighten up! Things are okay. It may seem dark, but it's not."

Now, thirty-six years later, we found ourselves in a similar position. We just kept waiting and watching the water. We kept looking around making sure everything was okay.

Everything began happening quickly. The water started coming in and kept filling in. The first thing my mom said, *again*, was, "Oh, the encyclopedias!" We had to go put those encyclopedias up, *again*, even though by now the information was outdated.

The only thing that went through my mind was that water should not be coming in—not *again*! I know it went through my sister's mind too—not *again*! We were doing this all over *again*, having to lift up these encyclopedias. However, we were reminded that God has a sense of humor. Here we were lifting the encyclopedias, yet *again*.

Plan B

As the water began to come in swiftly, we stayed in the dining room area. We did not even go into any other rooms.

We did not want to get pinned in by the furniture. Wooden furniture floats. My parents had a huge oak dining room table that was solid wood. It was big enough for all five of us in my parents' house to climb unto it. Yet, it was also heavy enough that it would not float as readily.

As the water deepened, we realized that our Plan A for quick evacuation was no longer viable. Our Plan B was if the water got too high, we would go ahead and climb into the attic. The stairs to the attic were in the garage. To get to the garage, we had to walk through the kitchen. It was time for Plan B.

As we walked through the house, we noticed the increased water level outside. When I opened the door to the garage, I observed how the water level was rapidly changing. I thought, "That's not a problem." But, as we began to move forward to exit out of the house, the exterior garage door suddenly buckled in one spot.

The door had been reinforced to hold, yet one of the side panels buckled just enough so that water could come rushing in. The force of the water carried everything that was in the garage crashing toward the kitchen door. Our path to the attic was blocked.

One of the things that obscured our path was a huge, old table saw that my dad had in the garage. He had gotten it right after hurricane Camille. The forceful water hurled it up against the door. It usually took my dad and my two brothers to move that big, old, heavy table saw. Even with three men, they were grunting. We could not move it, but the water could! The rushing water just moved it like it was nothing.

Numbly, we turned around to head back to the dining room. Because the table saw was in the way, we could not even close the door behind us. Since I was the first one at the garage door, I was the last to turn around to head back through the kitchen. As I walked through the doorway, the refrigerator fell on top of me. I was pinned between it and my parents butcher block. Even though the butcher block was solid wood, it did not float. It was too heavy. The refrigerator caught me on my leg. I could not push it away.

I hollered to Nick, "Nick, I'm pinned!" He came over to me, grabbed that refrigerator, and yanked it. I heard him grunt and he tossed it off me. He was only twelve years old. He had not had his growth spurt, yet. I am five feet six inches tall. He could stand next to me and I could put my chin on top of his head, if I stretched. Nevertheless, he moved that refrigerator. He saved me!

As the water rushed in from the garage, it was almost up to my waist. All we could think to do next was to climb up on the dining room table. We kept thinking that it was going to stop. It is going to stop. It will not come much higher. What else could we do?

We later discovered that God was watching out for us. In His good timing, He prevented us from going into the attic. My parents ended up with ten and a half feet of water in their home. If we had gone up into the attic, we would have drowned there.

The Angel

Back in the house, we returned to sit on the dining room table. How much higher will the water get? My sister and I picked a spot on the wall and decided that when the water got to that spot, we would get out of the house. At the time, we did not realize how high up the mark was that we chose. That knot was flush with the top of the window, which was about sixteen inches from the ceiling.

As the dining room table began to float on the water, surrounded by other swirling furniture, we watched the water hit the mark. We knew we had to escape. My father said, "It's my fault we're in here. I will get you out. I'll get you out."

Now, my dad had difficulty moving. He used to be five feet nine inches tall. Presently, at five feet six inches tall, I am the taller one. Due to the type of arthritis that he had and the condition of his spine, his center of gravity was now in his lower torso rather than in his upper body. He reminded me of Humpty Dumpty, especially in the water. When attempting to float, he would go upside down, with his feet sticking up.

I kept telling him, "I can do this Dad." I knew that I was the strongest swimmer. Nick was also a strong swimmer. I had full confidence in Nick's swimming capabilities. As a child I had received swimming instruction from Brother Albert, from St. Stanislav. From him, I learned all that I needed to know in order to take the lifeguard test. However, I stubbornly refused to "save" him, so I never took the test.

Years later, Brother Albert was still giving swimming lessons. He would drive up to the pool at St. Stanislav in his little golf cart. Nick was one of his last students before he finally retired. I helped Brother Albert teach Nick. What he and I did not teach Nick, Nick learned through scouting. So, Nick was extremely well trained. He was a very, very strong swimmer.

Nick was actually given the lifeguard test three times when he was twelve years old. He passed it every time. But, because he was so young, the instructor thought it was a fluke. They could not believe he could pass it. However, after the third time, they finally admitted he could do it. Nick also knew he could swim. He had the confidence.

As we found ourselves floating on the dining room table, we developed our next plan. I thought that we should go into the water and swim through the bay window in the front of the house. This was the biggest window. The back windows were higher and smaller. It would have been more difficult to exit through them. Also, the eaves on the house were lower by the bay window. Then, upon exiting the bay window, we would be able to grab hold of the eave of the house.

However, there was one problem with this plan. If you look at the bay window, it was obvious that Dad would not fit through it. He would be stuck in the window. The width of my dad was far greater than the width of the window. Thus, my dad thought we should go through the front door.

Nick and I swam through the water and pulled on the front door, but we could not get it open. Dad had locked it. Prior to the water coming in, my dad kept going in and out the front door to check on the storm. Each time, he would automatically lock the door. We kept saying, "Dad, do not lock the door. Do not lock the door! If you lock the door we won't get out."

Part of the problem was that water pressure had pushed the door in just enough so that we could not unlock the deadbolt. There was no way to push the door back when you are in the water. We thought if we could get to the outside, it might be easier because we could brace our feet and pull the door towards us, and then unlock it. In order to try that, we would have to get out through a window first. Nick and I swam toward the bay window.

Dad was still in the water, trying to get to the front door to pull on the handle. Not finding success, he went back to the table to be with my mom as she had been calling him. She wanted him beside her.

Then my mom said, "Okay, everybody, stop! I want you to all pray before you do anything else." It is weird the things that go through your mind. I thought of a football huddle. So, Nick and I huddled to pray.

My dad was brought up acknowledging St. Joseph as our patron saint. The St. Joseph's prayer card has a warning label on it. It says that all you need to do is just carry this card with you to be protected. You do not even have to read it. You just need to hold it, hear it, or say it. The very first thing mentioned is that you will not die by drowning. It has never been known to fail. This is one of the oldest prayers in church history. My dad had given each of his children a copy of this prayer to keep with them. He had one in his own wallet.

After Nick and I said Hail Mary and Our Father for our family in our little football huddle, we said the St. Joseph's prayer. Right afterwards, I said, "Okay! Break! Time-out! Let's get to work!"

My mom was already starting to panic. She was in shock. You could see it. My dad was starting to get a little unnerved, too, but not as bad. His panic was evidenced more as masculine, macho man irrationality. He felt that he had put his family in a terrible spot, so now he had to get them out. In reality, he could barely move, so there was no way he could do this. He had to depend on his two daughters, and his grandson.

My sister was even getting a little jumpy; but she was still staying levelheaded. She was staying right with my mom the entire time. She was not leaving her. We entered into a mode of "It's time to exit. It's time to leave." I had convinced my dad that we could do it.

I grabbed Nick and said, "This is what I want you to do. In order for Memaw and Pappa to leave, they are going to have to think that I have lost my mind. I'm going to send you, their grandson, their baby, out into the hurricane, by himself." I knew that this was the only way to get them to leave. They would follow Nick.

I told Nick, "This is how it's going to play out. I am going to send you out the window first. Then, I am going to send Memaw out to you. Next comes Aunt Pam. You put Aunt Pam with Memaw. Then I will send out Pappa. You stay right there. Then I'll come out." Well, it almost worked that way.

First, on the way to the window, I set the furniture up in a line. That way, when it came time for my sister to send my mom to the window, all she had to do was hold on to the furniture all the way down. It made an easier exit for her by creating a route to follow.

Next, I had Nick up there with me by the window. I was able to open the window easily. I attributed being able to get it open to two things. Number one was the good Lord. Number two, the fact that when we moved into that home back in 1979, dad and I had applied graphite to all the windows, so that when you opened them up, they would go up nice and easy and not squeakily. It only takes one application because the graphite glues to the window. It just came up for me like nothing. I kicked the screen out the window and it swept away.

I gently said to my mom, "I have to yank down the curtain, Mom." She said that would be fine. That was my irrationality, because it really did not matter. I just did not want to hurt my mom's feelings in yanking down her curtain that she had worked so hard to put up there. I quickly yanked it down so that it would be out of the way. The blinds, on the other hand, were too hard to pull down. After fighting with the drawstrings, I managed to pull them up.

Although Nick and I both dove into the water to get out, the others entered feet first. We can all dive, but it was easier for them to go feet first out of the window, and then float up, rather than to dive down and then turn and come up. Due to our training, it was easier for Nick and me to dive down.

After Nick went through the window, mom went into the water first. Outside the bay window was an overhang of about six feet, paralleling the ground, straight out from the house. The ceiling of this overhang was actually higher than the water level. As her feet went through the window and she came to the surface, she entered an alcove created by this overhang with a small air pocket. There was still surface tension on the water in this overhang area that allowed about six inches of airspace. She grabbed a breath of air, and bobbed back down into the water to travel another three feet in order to come out from under the overhang. When she arose from the water, she was disoriented. She felt hands grab her and pull her arm back to the overhang. That was Nick. He was there waiting.

When my sister went out next, she said that she could hear Nick yelling while she was still under water, "Over here. Over here." He was not screaming. He was very calm. He was a beacon to her when she was underneath the water.

Then, as Pam came out from under the water, he grabbed her and wrapped her around my mother. Nick's composure helped my sister to calm down immediately. My mother immediately became calm as well. He was not acting like a kid, but like a young man. This was our boy!

While this was going on, I kept swimming in and out, up from underneath, back and forth. I did not remember doing this, but my mother and sister said that I did. I was letting them know the progress of our dad. I do remember coming up and telling them, "I'm having trouble getting Dad out. I'm going back to try again."

It was very difficult. Dad kept trying to open up the front door. He knew he could not fit through the window. Dad and I were arguing the entire time. "I can do this! I can do this!" he said.

I said, "Dad, I'm doing this. I can do this. You trained me well. I know what I am doing. Let me do this for us. I am the swimmer in the family. You always said that I could swim underneath the water itself. As a kid, I terrified you all to death. I did not swim on top of the water until Brother Albert taught me. Otherwise, I swam underneath the water to the point that you thought I was drowned half the time. Now is my time. This is why I can swim underwater." I tried to explain to him that everything about me led up to this point in my life so that I could help my family. I had taught Nick how to swim hard and underneath the water like that too.

Finally, I said, "Dad, give me the key. I will try again to open the door from the front." I promised him that I would get him out. I said that if he gave me the key, I would get the door unlocked and get him out. He acquiesced and gave it to me.

I again swam through the window and to the surface to let mom and Pam know that, I was going to go around and unlock the front door for Dad because he said he could not fit through the window. I dove back underneath the water and around to the front door. I discovered something that Dad had forgotten to tell me. He had also locked the screen door for which there was no key, only an inside catch.

Unbeknownst to me, Nick calmly told my mom and sister, "You all stay here. I have to go help my mom." He said that as though he was just going to help grandpa with the groceries. Next thing I know, Nick was right beside me. He and I both started yanking on the screen door to pop the lock. We could not do it.

The water we swam through that day was very strange. You could not see very far because it was like swimming in brackish water. Yet, you could still see daylight in it. Normally, you could see a little, but not that brightly. With it being overcast, it should not have been that light. The wide overhang from the house should have cast a shadow. It should not have been reflecting any type of light.

Yet, it was like daylight and sunshine in that water. That is how bright it was. You could not actually see rays of sunlight, but it was as though sunshine was coming through. The sky was darkened. It was similar to twilight. It was like whatever light was present, was being magnified three times.

I thought the brightness might be because salt water is clearer than fresh water. We were definitely in very salty water. In addition, you could not see any debris floating out in front of us. If you looked down into the water you could not even see knee-deep, yet somehow, we could see through it.

At that point in time, the surface tension on the water underneath the overhang, in the air pocket, was breaking. It was filling up with water fast. There was only a three inch gap, just enough in which to stick our noses. We swam to the surface.

Nick said, "Mom, we've got to go. We have to go now. Pappa is going to have to make it on his own. He's in God's hands." Nick forced me look at him. Here I am, looking at this twelve-year-old young man, who is speaking volumes of wisdom to me. I realized that my young son was right. This was the second time that he saved me.

Nick and I swam over to my sister and my mom. I told them that we could not get dad out. I said that he had locked both doors. Just as our words had finished, and we were starting to edge our way along the eave of the house, around the side, toward the back, my dad came popping up through the flood, streams of water spewing everywhere.

When my dad bobbed up in the water, Nick let go of the roof and free swam to my dad despite the strong current. You could see a deep whirlpool at the corner of the house. I let go of the roof, but I stayed close to that overhang in order to grab hold of it, as that current was pulling me. Nick swam through it as though it was nothing. He grabbed my dad because he could see that he was being sucked right back down under the overhang. Nick grabbed hold of dad and put his hands up on the roof, too. Now, all five of us were hanging on to the edge of the overhang.

Dad said that he saw the Archangel Michael come to him and yank him through that window. He said that he could tell his lungs were filling with water. He felt hands on both sides of him pushing him through the window. It was the Archangel Michael, coming to save him!

Trinity

Nick stayed right by my dad and free swam near him the entire time in the front of our line. As we moved along the roof and got to the corner, my dad was ready to give up. Nick kept saying, "Don't Pappa! Don't Pappa! Hold on!"

Just then, a huge handmade door that happened to be off the shed of my dad's only living brother who lived right next door, came floating toward us. It was a big door, big enough for all five of us to grasp. It got caught in the whirlpool. I told Nick to watch when it flung out of the whirlpool and seize it. We had to snatch it at that moment, or we'd lose it. If we grabbed it right then, we would have it. We were able to secure it and pull it up to us. It was just long enough for all five of us to line up along it.

We lined up in this order: my sister, my mom, Nick, my dad, and me. That is how we were hanging onto the door. Then, I recalled something that I had told my sister earlier, when she called the day before to say that Dad refused to leave. I had told her that she could take care of mom, that I would take care of dad and that Nick would float in between. How true those words had become!

While the others held tightly onto the door, Nick and I maneuvered it, dragging it along the side of the house to get it around to the back of the house so that we could climb up onto the lower portion of the roof. Nick kept my dad afloat the entire time. Every time my dad started going under, Nick would pull him back up. As the water kept rising, Nick kept nudging the door.

Finally, we got to the back roof. From this lower portion of the roof, we could easily move to a higher portion if we needed to, when the winds changed. Nick clambered out of the water and pulled each one of us up onto the roof. He hauled everyone up. That little kid got us up there.

First, he got my sister, and then my mom. He manhandled my dad who weighed over three hundred pounds up onto that roof. Finally, he helped me up. Nick stayed calm. He kept all of us calm. Nick and I wedged that door against the roof to use as a platform. This gave my dad something to use for his footing. Otherwise, my dad would have slid straight back down into the water.

Up on the roof, we knew we were safe. We knew God was present with us. The winds were fairly calm. There was one piece of Styrofoam that came blowing by and hit my mom and dad on the head, but that was it. Once we were all on top of the roof and we knew we were safe, Nick turned back into a twelve-year-old boy, back into being his usual self.

As I have said before, God has a sense of humor. He will put something in there to calm you down. From nowhere, a boat came floating up onto the back of the property. I said, "Dad, do you think we could charge a docking fee?"

He said, "Yeah, if it stays there, we can!" We always find a way, something to get us to laugh. Later on, the boat floated away. I told everyone that now the neighbors would get to charge the docking fee.

My mom was concerned about my brother. She was afraid that he and his wife had drowned in their house since we did not see them up on their roof. I told her, "Mom, they are high and dry. They are safe in the platform he built in his attic with their two puppies. The water level in his house is not nearly as high as it is in your house. His roof is much higher, as well."

My mom calmly asked, "Do you believe that?"

I said, "Yes, I know it. I know that's where Joe is."

At least while we sat on the roof, it was not raining. Then, God sent us another sign that we could not ignore. We saw two birds fly by with a third following them. That is the symbol for the Trinity in nature. We saw three birds fly by in this formation. This was a sign for us and it was especially comforting for Nick. Nick knew we would be okay because his Heavenly Father was there. Yes, He was there!

Actually, I would honestly go through the storm again. My sister called for our help at just the right time. If she had waited even a half hour later, we would have been gone. Once you hit those roads during an evacuation, there is no way to turn back.

I would go through it again for the blessing I received, a glimpse of the man my son would become. I told my husband that if I were to go to the grave today, I would be all right, because I know who Nickolas will be. Having a taste of the future man my son will become, was the best gift I could ever be given!

Now What?

as told by Annette Richard

Signs and Wonders

We stayed on the roof until the water receded, which was most of the day, five to six hours. By late afternoon, when the water got low enough, my younger brother came out of his house, which was behind my parents' home. He was dry until he hit what was left of the water. He stopped suddenly and went back into his house. When he again walked outside, we noticed that he had grabbed his little shotgun. Snakes were a concern. The ravine was well known for housing water moccasins.

My brother went into the garage and grabbed the extension ladder. He brought it over to where we were on the roof so we could all climb down. Once off the roof, we decided to walk to the hospital, which was only a quarter of a mile away.

As we walked along the road to the hospital, we noticed other little signs that spoke to us like the three birds flying overhead during the storm had done. The things that we saw comforted us. We knew we were fine. Our job had been to get out of the house and get up on the roof. We had done that.

One reassuring sight was my dad's little statues on his porch. They were all swept away except for the St. Joseph statue. It was still in place just where he always kept it. It never moved. My mom's Blessed Mother statue was sitting there, just fine. No problem. My sister's statue was lying down, as if someone had just picked it up and gently laid it over.

My parents' home was built on family land. The original homestead, owned by my father's parents, was no longer there. However, my grandparents' statue remained. As kids, we used to play "Ring Around the Rosie" and "Tag" around the statue. We would play all kinds of games around it. Many a time, we grabbed it just before it hit the ground because it was not on a very sturdy pedestal.

After the storm, it was still standing on the very same pedestal in the very same location. We all walked by and looked at it and we knew He had been there; because, it had not moved, not in all of those strong currents. The statue was still sitting there, Mary with her arms open to us.

We continued walking up the road. The first person that we ran into was my sister's high school boyfriend who also happened to be the first person we ran into after Camille.

After Camille, he deliberately came over to check on us, as he was my sister's boyfriend. They never married, but remained close. During Katrina he was staying at the home of his younger brother who lived behind my parents. The last time he lent my mother a jacket. This time he lent her a jacket again to keep her warm because she was chilly.

My mom knew that we were all okay, but she was showing signs of shock. Since Nick's presence helped my mom to feel calm, my sister made sure that mom could always see Nick. Nick would look to see if he could see my mom as well. That helped her to stay focused with what we were doing. If her grandbaby was okay, she was okay. Of my parents' four grandchildren, Nick is the youngest, and he is their precious, their little gem. Because of Katrina, they have become even closer to Nick.

When we arrived at the hospital, mom was checked out. They gave her a little blanket. Then, they transported us to Bay High School. The person who transported us to the high school was one of the county supervisors. I said to him, "David, I don't know how Cooper is. Can you find out?"

He said, "Where is he?" I told him that Cooper was at the house. The look on his face—David's heart was on his face. You see, what David was doing was going around collecting various family members. Not all of them were alive. He reassured me, "Cooper's made it. He is Strong. He is too stubborn. I know he made it. He always said that the good Lord does not want him and the devil is scared of him! He is going to be okay! It will take more than this, more than a little water to keep him from being around." I asked him to just let me know, to just get word to me.

Before the water started coming in my parent's home, I had been able to stay in touch with Cooper through landlines. We even had electrical power, until the wind got strong. In a storm like this when the wind reaches a certain speed, the power company shuts down.

The last time I spoke with Cooper, water had not yet come in. My sister was the last one to talk with my husband. As the water started coming in, the landlines went dead. Now, I could not find out how he was.

What I did not know at the time, was that someone had put out a huge sign in our neighborhood that said, "Where's Cooper?" Everybody around there knows Cooper. We have a Cooper Junior, but there is only one Cooper. Word eventually got back to me that yes, Cooper was spotted. He was okay. He had a few scratches, and was "a little bit" hurt. I felt a little panicky, until I could find out how "little" he was hurt. I was not sure what "a little bit" meant.

We were at the high school for several days. The conditions were horrible. There was no water. My sister was able to get up into her attic and retrieve some sleeping bags that were dry, out of one of her storage containers. My mom and dad were able to lay down on those. Nick and I roughed it. We were used to it with all the years of scouting. We were in the same clothes for several days. We did not get new clothes until the church groups started sending them.

One day, my dad, still in his swim trunks, questioned, "I don't understand. Why did I make it? Why am I still here?" I asked dad if he had his wallet on him. He said that he did. He always had his wallet with him. I told him to look in his wallet.

He gave me a questioning look as if to say, what do you know that I am supposed to know? Then he remembered. He was already starting to smile and chuckle as he pulled out his wallet. He removed his St. Joseph's prayer card. I told him to look at the back. He said he knew. I told him that he had it on him the whole time. I said, "You were the one who told me, and my sister, and my brothers to always carry that card, and you'll be protected." Pleased, he chuckled, as he knew I remembered.

A few days later, after we had time to process what we had experienced during the storm, Nick shared with me, "Mom, if it hadn't been for my faith and Boy Scouts, I would not have been able to do what I did. God gave me faith that I could do this. Scouts gave me the confidence I needed, so I knew I could do it." He also shared that if priests could get married, he would become one in a heartbeat!

After four weeks, with great relief, I finally saw Cooper for myself. He had gotten a little bump on the head, but he was fine. By the time I saw him, he was working a few hours each day for the County. Then he, like other county workers, would come home and work on mucking out our house, getting rid of the debris and the mud and water, down to the sheet rock.

As we gradually cleaned up our home, we saw signs of God's presence. He left His little marks here and there. This confirmed what we knew all along during the hurricane—God was with us.

When Cooper left our house before the storm, he had tried to grab our cat on the way out, but she would not come. She was okay, however. She floated on the furniture. He could see the little paw prints everywhere when he went back in.

What was so miraculous, and I do say miraculous, was something else we discovered in our home. I had had an open curio cabinet with a number of little resin statues that I would use on cakes. I would use them, clean them up, and return them to storage in the open curio cabinet. They were mostly for St. Joseph's altar cakes. They were resin and should have floated. They did not. They all stayed in the open cabinet. They stayed in place.

I have several religious portraits such as *The Last Supper*, *The Holy Family*, the child Jesus, and a huge crucifix. All of them were hanging up on the walls. All of them had blessed palms behind them. When I was able to come back into the house, they were all where they had been left as if nothing had touched them. Mold was already growing on the walls, but nothing anywhere near these portraits. The palms were still behind everything.

One of my pictures was of the child Jesus when He was about twelve. It had been framed and given to me by my father. He had given one to each of his children. The only damage to the back of it was the age damage that had already been there. There is no evidence that it was ever under water. That was the way with all these portraits. My dad had framed all of them when I was a child. It was just awesome to see that they were all like this! My sisters' were the same way.

In my younger brother's case, there is a story behind his portrait all its own. We all went into his home, which is directly behind my parent's home right after the water receded. He had a beautiful chandelier hanging over his dining room table. When we walked in, above where his dining room table *was*, the chandelier was gone with just wires hanging in its spot. Connected to those wires, unharmed, as if someone had just picked it up and hung it there, was his picture of *The Last Supper*. I jokingly told my younger brother, "He's telling you, you need to rebuild and build Him a new table. Build a new home. That's His message to you right there because He put *The Last Supper* right over where your dining room table should be."

One day we were able to check on Our Lady of the Woods Shrine. When I was a kid, if I was troubled by what

48

was going on, I would always go there. After Camille, we went in there to clean up and sweep off the leaves that were around. After Katrina, we went to do the same thing.

It just so happens that the day we got there the National Guard was there cleaning up trees etc. We asked a guardsman how the shrine had fared. He said that he just had to take a broom and sweep her off. She was totally unharmed.

We pray to the Blessed Mother and ask her to beseech her Son for us. We pray to Him, but we ask her to put in a good word for us. That is because whenever she asked her Son for something He would say, "Yes, Mom!" She is special to us. She is our hope. Hope is what we needed right after the storm.

Oh, and Nick's PlayStation? It actually made it through the hurricane. It had a little moisture in it, but not seawater. It survived. Finally, he wore it out. It gave way last Christmas, so we bought him a new PlayStation.

Tough Times

It is good we had our faith, because initially, our contact with FEMA was not good. After hurricane Camille, things ran very smoothly. At that time, the National Guard's mission was designed to take care of natural disasters like this. We could call on each other's states, and they would be here. Boom! With Katrina, it's more like, "Let's see if our troops have been deployed or not. If they haven't been, we can send them to you."

It was very disappointing. We heard from family and friends and people in other states, that truckers had goods from other states ready to bring to us that were held up for weeks, because FEMA didn't want to come in.

I experienced this first hand. FEMA was here two days after the storm hit. Everybody had evacuated to the school, even though it had been hit by water as well. This was our fallout shelter. The school was where we went after Hurricane Camille, also.

I was helping out the county workers at the high school. The workers included those from the county welfare department. A FEMA representative told them, "We are leaving. We are not coming back. It's not safe for us here." What about us? That is when the police opened up businesses and we went in and grabbed canned goods.

Our days at the high school ended when my older brother came over to retrieve us and took us to his office at the Jack C. Stennis Space Center. He quietly took us out there, as it was only supposed to be refuge for the immediate family, meaning his wife, his parents, and his daughter. However, he figured out a way to get us all out there.

When we left for the test site, the timing was good. People were starting to get violent at the high school. There was nothing there. No food and no water. Our first responders happened to be church groups and the few national guardsmen they could muster up. Hancock County was the worst, because we had become an island, cut off from everything. People wondered why we just did not leave before the storm hit.

A number of people stayed, because like us, they went through Camille. Why not stay through Katrina? This storm was only to be a category three when it hit. The winds were not bad. We were out walking around in it. If it had not been for the water, we would have been okay.

Here in Hancock County, the water went fourteen miles inland. This was the only place where it went that far inland. You heard on the news about Biloxi. You heard on the news about New Orleans. But, you didn't hear anything in the middle about Hancock County. It was as if we did not exist. That was true. We did not exist, anymore!

According to everything that I have heard from friends who work in Harrison Country Civil Defense, the water came into Bay St. Louis and flopped around all of the edges. It plopped onto the land. When it roared back in, one's location determined how many times you were hit by the water, which built up with each wave. Some places just had three feet; some had eight feet. Those that were really slammed had thirty-five plus feet. It just depended. My parents had ten and a half feet and were hit by the water twice. Just one-fourth of a mile up the road at the hospital, they had four and a half feet. That is walking distance. It just depended, literally, on your location.

Another thing we were told about the storm was that at the same time the hurricane hit, we were supposed to have had an earthquake, sixty miles out from the mouth of the Mississippi River with a magnitude of five. This would mean that we were smacked with a tsunami. That is why it went fourteen miles inland.

I went online to try to find out about it. I tried every query I could think of to find this information. The best I could find was if you do a search on earthquakes for 2005, it immediately takes you to sites about Hurricane Katrina. However, there is no mention of an earthquake. So why the online link?

I have pictures of the waves that came in from a student at St. Stanislaus. They had not evacuated because they were a very well-fortified school. It looks just like the tsunami that hit Somalia. It was not just one wave, but also a series of waves from thirty-five feet to sixty feet.

Another curious thing we learned afterward, concerned the Spanish Acres area, on Old Spanish Trail. It did not get flooded. All of us started laughing and joking about it; because, due to the way the roads and ditches were constructed, if it just rained, it flooded. That tells you it was a dry storm. The one subdivision that floods if you turn on a garden hose was high and dry!

Another perplexing thing was the odor up in the bay compared to out by our house. The smell at the bay was strangely different. The smell of the mud by our house smelled just like the mud after Camille. It is as if that scent was burned into your memory. However, the smell in the bay was different. My dad, who was former military and who had been around decomposing bodies, said that it smelled like dead bodies in the bay.

For a while it was thought that we were dead. It was reported that my dad had died. It turned out it was another gentleman for whom he had been named. My husband lost one cousin. One of her sons found her. Her sons had peace with that because she had been in a lot of physical pain prior to the storm. She had been racked with it. Painkillers were not even helping her. For them it had been a blessing, because they knew she had gone home.

There were a lot of people that we know of who died, but are still just listed as missing. They are not reported among the dead. We have some very close doctor friends who have told us that the numbers that were released as dead are really only the dead who were identified.

Nick and I continued to stay at St. Stanislaus until October 30, when we got a FEMA trailer. The people at the test site were wonderful. They were great. They provided food for us. There were a lot of MREs, (meals ready to eat) but that's okay. It was food! I ended up working for them a few hours each day as a shelter manager. At the facility, they ran a typical summer space camp program for the kids since they were out of school. Nick got to take advantage of this opportunity. If it hadn't been for the storm, Nick would not have been able to go to space camp. Nickelodeon also brought a crew out there for the kids to enjoy, including SpongeBob.

When we finally got a FEMA trailer, we were able to put it on our property. The first one we had was a little bitty Cavalier, the one with all the formaldehyde issues. Then, we switched to the mini FEMA mobile home. It was a full mobile home, but it was a short one. It was forty feet long, not seventy or eighty feet long. It was a handicapped model with a big bathroom and small living room and kitchen, one decent sized bedroom and one itty-bitty bedroom. That is what we lived in for a while. Now, we are living back in our home, but it still needs work. It has not been easy to try to get any money to rebuild our home.

Another issue has been health concerns. My mom's cancer had been considered in remission before the storm. The cancer was down to almost where they could not see it. It was down to the size of about a quarter. It was still inoperable, but she was doing well. It came back when she was in a FEMA trailer. They could not stop it. She has since passed away.

Other members of our family have struggled with respiratory problems and staph infections like crazy. These were the same kind of staph infections that had been reported that fishermen were getting. Before the storm, my husband had gotten it twice when he worked on a particular section of the beach with the beach patrol. After the hurricane, it did not matter.

We were told that the DuPont chemical facility did not have a spill. Yet, realistically, it was submerged under water. Get real! We had chemical burns. I have taught chemistry. I have had OSHA training. I am a certified OSHA safety specialist. I know what chemical burns look like.

Nick and I have also both suffered from heavy hair loss. The hair loss became an even bigger issue when we lived in a FEMA trailer because of the additional chemicals to which we were exposed. Our hair was falling out by the clumps. It is coming back now.

It has been a long road. Despite it all, I believe in something a guy I know said. "To live in paradise you have to put up with a few little things." That is the price. Everyone who comes to this area really wants to have a second home here.

As a kid growing up, I could not wait to leave. I did for a while, but I have moved back. This is really a good place to raise children and have a family. There may not be as many activities or things to do, but there are plenty of family activities like going to the beach or camping or fishing.

At the first year anniversary of the storm, I received a phone call from my mom, my dad and my sister, separately, to thank me, and especially to thank Nick, because they would not be here if it had not been for him.

When you came down to it, I could not have done it by myself. Nick was the man of the hour. He was on top of it. His presence made you feel that things were going to be okay. He kept us calm. If it were not for Nick, I know my dad would not have made it, much less me. To continue to live in this paradise, we needed a hero. His name was Nick.

"Secrets"

Gifts, talents, uncovered	Sacrifices, time ticking, ticking, ticking
Bringing back the fun in life	Illusions create reality
Trust reinvested	Trust reinvested
People reconnecting through crisis	Transition quietly shining for onlookers
Recapture the pleasures, passions of the past	Vision blurred, hearing more acute, taste buds reawakened
Books destroyed, history put on hold	Books destroyed, history put on hold
Dreams taken to the sky, projects in process, success expected	Heroes honored, bravery recorded
A glimpse of a quiet vision	Pursue and follow your dream
Fantasies create wonders	Fantasies create wonders

The Hardest Part

as told by Nickolas Greene

The Storm

With news of the approaching hurricane, our family discussed what to do. My uncle, my father's brother, did not want to leave. So, my dad was going to stay with him. My mom and I were going to leave right away and go to Batesville, Mississippi, to stay with relatives. But that plan changed with a phone call from my aunt, my mother's sister. She told my mom, "Annette, Mom and Dad aren't going to leave."

My mom told her that she and I would come over to help. Mom said, "I'll take dad. You take mom, and Nick will float in between." We later learned the irony of these words as they became true.

After we arrived at my grandfather's house, my mom, my aunt Pam, my grandparents and I got everything set. We stocked up on food. We had the bare essentials. We were preparing for the worst. My grandfather, being military, wanted everyone to stay awake in case we needed to get out. Unfortunately, he also decided to lock the door. That was future problem number one.

I started to get sleepy, so I lay down on the couch. I thought, "Okay, so it's another storm. I slept through Hurricane Andrew. There were some other storms I slept through." I told myself that it was not that big of a deal. Even when the storm actually hit, we initially thought that everything was normal for the hurricanes we get. Everything could go on just fine.

We started hearing the wind. I reminded myself that I had been through this before. Even when the water started to trickle in the house, I knew this was expected. During a storm, the water just comes in, but not too high. We called up our families, asking, "How's everybody doing over there?" Stuff like that. I called up my dad.

Then, the water started to come in faster. It was getting higher and higher in the house. We tried not to be too worried, but we were. We had a plan to go to the attic if it got too deep. To get into the attic, we had to go through the garage, which sits a little lower than the rest of the house. The garage door had been closed before any water started coming in.

When the water got to be four feet high, I was starting to worry. The water was at the bottom of the window. I was okay, but I was worried. I was really getting worried now. Everybody was starting to get a little bit panicky. My mom and I were trying to keep a cool head. I was like, "Okay everybody—stay calm, stay calm!"

As the water climbed higher in the room, my mom decided that we should consider getting into the attic. She walked through the water, toward the kitchen, to get to the garage to check out the entrance to the attic. This spot was the weakest point in the house. The water literally ripped open the main garage door.

When that door popped open, I wondered, "What are we going to do? What are we going to do?"

I noticed mom standing in the doorway between the kitchen and the garage, right beside the refrigerator. I saw a wall of water, a perfect rectangle, coming from the garage door, coming straight at me. The next thing that I become aware of was that the refrigerator had lifted up and landed on top of my mom. (Mom later said that she had this feeling like she was about to die come over her.)

Mom called out, "Help! Help! Help!" I went over to help my mom get the refrigerator off her. I pushed it right side up, and mom got out. The refrigerator did not seem heavy at all for me! I felt strong that day. I felt afraid for my mom and everybody else, but not really for myself.

Once the water completely leveled out, I went back over to the garage and saw that everything had floated over to the attic stairs. We could not get to the attic. Everything stacked itself perfectly. There were two lawnmowers piled up there, plus other things from the garage. I could not move anything. I could not budge any of it and I was the strongest one in the family. I closed the door to the garage.

Now we started to feel anxious because the water was halfway up the walls. We all started to plan, "What are we going to do? What are we going to do?" Then my mom had a plan.

We had already tried to get out the front door, but my grandfather had locked it. The pressure between the door and the screen door prevented it from being pushed in even to try to unlock it. I told my mom to just forget it as it would not work. Pappa told her the same thing.

So, then mom dove into the water and opened up a window. She told me that I was going down and out the window first. When I asked why, she said that if I went first, then Memaw and Pappa would follow. I was prepared to do whatever it took to help my family.

It was very dark inside the house now. The water was dark too. It looked murky—like brackish water. I dove down into it with my eyes open, but I could not find the window. I came back up and told my mom I could not locate the window. She said to follow her leg. I tried again and this time I found it.

I swam through the window and popped up in the overhang of the roof where there was a pocket of air. I waited for just a little bit. I was thinking, "Where is everyone? Am I all alone?" Then I dove down again, popped up outside the house, and grabbed the roof. I started calling for the rest of my family. I said, "Here I am. Come on. Come on over here. Here I am."

Next, Memaw popped up. Then came my aunt Pam. I told my aunt Pam to stay right with Memaw. I was going to go see what I could do to help mom.

Mom said that she was having trouble getting Pappa out the window. She said she was going to try the front door again, but from the outside this time. It was not opening from this side either. I told her that we had to go. I told her that the air pocket would not last forever.

As we came up through the water with Memaw and Aunt Pam, I saw Pappa's feet bob up and then his head. Mom and I both swam over to get him. Then, what mom said earlier came true. We were all lined up, and I was floating between Memaw and Pappa!

Rooftop Revelations

Eventually, we pulled ourselves over to a low part of the roof. I climbed up and pulled Aunt Pam and Memaw up onto the roof, too. Then I tried to get Pappa up onto the roof. It was really hard. While I pulled him, mom was pushing on him from the water. We finally did it. Then mom climbed up on the roof, too.

There we all sat in a corner of the roof. I could feel a stinging, like rocks were being thrown at me. It was the sand and pieces of the roof shingles flying at us. We crawled to the other side of the roof to try to get away from it and it helped a little bit.

After we were all safe on the roof, I bawled and bawled. I started to think, "I could've died. I just could have died! I could have drowned! Why didn't I die?" Then, as I calmed down, I looked up at the sky. In the clouds I saw a face that reminded me of my other grandmother who had passed away. That helped me to feel better.

As we sat on the roof for hours, a boat floated up on the property. We started to joke about charging the owner rent to dock his boat there. We all started to laugh. Humor helped us.

The view from the roof made me think of the Everglades. All you could see were trees sticking up through the water. Everywhere you looked, that was all you could see. I did not want to get off the roof down into that water. There were water moccasins and alligators in the streams and creeks around here.

As the water went down, I realized we could not get off the roof, as we were too high. Then I saw my uncle, who lived in the house right behind my grandparents, come walking out of his house into the water towards us. He was holding a shotgun over his head army style. I wondered why he had a shotgun. Then I remembered the things in the water. He got a ladder for us to get down from the roof.

Life after the Storm

After we clambered down from the roof, we walked through the house but soon left. We walked down the road to the hospital. From there, they sent us to Bay High School. We stayed there for about a week. It was not too good. All the power was out. There were no working bathrooms. Everyone kept looking for bathrooms. People were anxious and angry.

After a week, my uncle was able to get in and find us. He took us to his office at Jack C. Stennis Space Center. We stayed there for several weeks. It certainly was not normal life, but I made some good friends there. It turned out to be one of the best things that happened to us.

After a while, a temporary school was opened for the kids. Although I had just turned thirteen, I joined the high school group as one of the younger students. One of the things we studied was chemistry. We got to take some great trips. Everyone got along. My mom got a job helping out there. Things were not too bad.

Then we got a tiny FEMA trailer so we could move "home." Things went from bad to worse to worst. The trailer was just too tiny for me. The bunk bed in my bedroom had a weight limit of 140 pounds. I weighed 180 pounds. The bed was made from plywood, with balsa wood like material for the platform.

The first night I slept on it I woke up with a bad crick in my neck. I realized that my shoulder had gone through the bottom of the bed. I tried to sleep on it anyway, but my body was just too big for that bunk. My shoulders were too wide.

So I thought, "Screw that!" I went to sleep on the sofa. I opened it up and lay down. The metal ribs on the bed poked me in the back.

We also had a lot of fleas while we were in that little trailer. They were a type of sand flea that seemed to be really common after the storm. I would be sitting there and they would start biting my ankles. I would smack at my legs and yell for them to get off me. I started to get angry.

I would go outside and look where my house had been. I just wanted my home. I wanted my home back. Not just the house, I wanted my home.

I became angry all the time. At school, other kids were angry too. Fights broke out all the time. I felt very edgy. All the kids were edgy and angry. The slightest thing would work on someone's nerves.

Lots of kids had other stories too. I would listen to their stories. Some of them had it worse than me. Others would tell their story and I would think, "You thought that was bad? I almost died! I could have drowned! Yeah, right, you had it tough." That made me angry. Sometimes, it was just too much to hear.

Also, I was sick frequently. I got many colds. I had respiratory problems. I was often tired. I wanted people to just let me alone and not bother me.

Then, one day at school, I realized that I still had my pocketknife in my backpack from scouting the past weekend. So, I did what I thought was the right thing. I turned my knife over to one of my teachers, who then turned it into the office. Because of that, the school administrator was going to expel me.

After my parents talked with administration, it was obvious that I was only trying to be honest. I was told that my honesty was appreciated. Instead of being expelled, I was sent to an alternative school for nine weeks. That is how I was thanked.

I changed. I became a very different person. This school was full of thugs and drug pushers. My experience here affected my thinking. It changed who I was. The biggest thing is that I did not trust anyone. This was not like me at all. I was very happy-go-lucky and trusting of anyone. Now, if someone came up to me, I would ask what it was they wanted from me. I just did not have faith in anyone. I was very angry all the time.

Then, we got a bigger FEMA trailer. This one was not much better. At least it did not have the formaldehyde issues like the old, small one. I still just wanted my home.

Road to Home

The second semester of my next school year, eighteen months after the storm, my parents decided to send me to St. Stanislaus as a boarding student. They felt living there would help me feel more like I was home. They thought the structure would be good. It did help. I liked it better there than at my regular high school. I still would occasionally get picked on by some kids, but I could handle that.

The day I began to be less angry and return to the person I am, was the day we could move back into our home. I began to trust again. Our home still needs some work, but we are living in our home again. The anger started to leave that day.

I am not exactly sure what the future holds. I know that I want to go on for further education after high school. In the immediate future, I am hoping to go to Australia with the People-to-People Student Ambassador program. Also, I really want to learn to SCUBA dive.

Looking back, I know that what helped me be able to save my family was Scouts. Boy Scouts had prepared me. I knew what to do, and how to do it. I would go through the storm again any day rather than deal with the aftermath. I could handle the storm. Having gone through it, I have five different solutions of what we could have done. I know what to do in that situation. But living in that FEMA trailer, and going through all the struggles for years afterward—that was the hardest part.

"Invitation"

Experience the power
Mother Nature has to offer

Help us to set the stage for
the event that is about to
befall us

Fill the bathtubs and sinks
with water for boiling

Stay awake

Pack the cars with important
papers, clothes and other
essentials for at least one
week

Gas up cars, trucks and be
ready to move in an instant,
find the flashlight, candles,
and such

Stay calm

Moms and Dads, as Katrina
hits, hold tight to your
children, cuddle babies

Safety of all concerned must
be paramount

Bring canned goods, small
items to eat, bottled water
that can be stored

Keep freezer door closed to
save food for days to come

Stay awake

Take care of the family pets;
see to it that none are left
behind

Quickly, quickly every
second will mark moments
in our lives

Stay calm

Reassure the elders, strength
has to come from you;
strength has to come from
me

Families visiting friends
gathering together for meals,
long talks, and great
moments of silence

Being together once more

Families visiting, friends
gathering together, flowers
presented, gifts appreciated,
thank you's extended

Being together once more

Strength of Family
as told by Mike Kovasevich

Lost History

Hurricane Katrina was eight hours that changed the coast forever. As one of the oldest cities in the country, Biloxi lost a lot of history. Our family lost some of our personal history as well, but we were lucky to still have our home.

My mother's house sits right next door to mine. That is where I grew up with my brothers and sisters and my mom and dad. I was one of ten children. My mother had three sets of twins! Every five years she had another set of twins. When the last set of twins was born, she also had a one-year-old, a three-year-old, a set of five-year-old twins, one of whom was me, a seven-year-old, and ten-year-old twins. That is when those old cloth diapers were around. You would be out in the yard playing in the mud and those cloth diapers would be hanging to your knees, soaking wet.

There were always about thirty or forty people at my parents' house when I was growing up, because everybody would bring their friends over. This was actually the entertainment center because the schoolyard was right next door. The school yard was where we played football, baseball

71

etc. Back then, this was one of those spots to be in the summer.

The house I live in now, right next door to my parents, was built by my grandparents. My grandmother, on my mother's side, was one of the youngest of twenty-three children. They were all born in Louisiana. My grandmother moved here to Biloxi with her parents when she was a preteen for work in the seafood factories. By the time she moved to Biloxi, many of her older brothers and sisters had already married and had children of their own, so they remained in Louisiana. Eventually, my grandmother married my grandfather who ended up owning one of the factories.

This part of town, called Old Biloxi, is where all the seafood factories used to be. Now, it is mostly casinos. Where you see all the casinos now, there used to be seafood factories. Back in the late 1800s and early 1900s, Biloxi was considered the seafood capital of the world. There were more shrimp and oysters coming out of Biloxi than there was anywhere in the world. Almost all of Biloxi was factories. Everyone who worked in the factories lived right around here as well.

Living close to the factories created an interesting system for being called to work. You would know around three or four o'clock in the morning if you had work that day, because the factory that had shrimp coming in would blow a steam whistle. Each factory's whistle had a different tone. You would listen for the whistles; and if you heard the whistle for your factory, you knew you had to go to work that day.

Today, many of the older people in their eighties, used to work in those factories before school when they were kids. The whistle would blow so they would get up and go to work

72

till about eight o'clock in the morning. Then, they would walk over to St. Michael's to go to school. When they got out of school, they would go back to the factories to finish up for the day. This was how the kids helped their parents.

Most people working in the factories would head shrimp. The heads of the shrimp would be thrown in a bucket, and then it would be weighed. Each person was paid like five cents a pound, whatever the going rate was. In Biloxi, the nickels became famous, because they were called shrimp nickels. You could tell they came from the factory, because the acid from the shrimp would tarnish the nickels. All the nickels in Biloxi looked like pennies because they were tarnished.

Many of the people here in Biloxi came from France and Yugoslavia. When the factories first started there were not enough workers living here to support the plants. So, those who were here were asked if they had any relatives living in the old country who might be willing to relocate.

My relatives came here from Yugoslavia. Today, their homeland is called Croatia. Where they came from was primarily small fishing villages. Thousands came over from Croatia by the boatload and settled here.

That is when my great aunts and uncles came and settled in Biloxi. My grandfather was one of the younger ones in the family. So he stayed behind. When things got bad in Croatia, or Yugoslavia, he decided to meet relatives in the USA and live over here. Previously, they had all come over in groups, but he traveled by himself. They came in through New York and then to New Orleans and then to Biloxi. My grandfather came by a different route.

My grandfather got on a ship that took him to Italy. From Italy, he was supposed to come New Orleans and then to Biloxi. Trouble arose when he got to Havana, Cuba, and was supposed to switch ships for one bound to New Orleans. Well, he could not speak Spanish and he could not speak English so he boarded the wrong boat. He ended up in Mexico!

He stayed there and made a life for himself. He found employment on the oil docks. He married a Mexican Indian and had three sons. One of those sons was my dad. When my dad was twelve years old, they sent him to stay with family here in Biloxi for a better education.

The problem was they would not let him cross the border. He had all kinds of trouble. Actually, he had to lie about his age. He said he was fourteen rather than twelve. A United States senator stepped in and got involved. I had all the paperwork documenting the event, but the storm took that away. I did have all the letters that were written from immigration, etc., but they are gone.

Finally, they let him come across on one condition. His aunts and uncles who he had come to live with were not to be his legal guardians. The parish priest was to be his guardian. So, he arrived to live with the family here in Biloxi, speaking no English. But, he adapted and eventually married my mom. Now we have family in Croatia and in Mexico.

It was funny, two days after the storm, I spoke to a photographer from Germany, who asked to take a picture of a sign I had made from the debris. I had found some spray paint and wrote a message on the board that said, "Keep out or be shot!" I nailed that sign to the debris.

After giving him permission to take the photograph, he told me that the picture would be going all over the world that night. I asked him to hold on a minute. I got the can of spray paint and I wrote, "Kovacevich is okay!" I nailed that sign to a tree and told him I needed him to send out that picture all over the world tonight as well. Sure enough, my relatives in Croatia saw it and called us!

Evacuate?

People ask why I would stay for a hurricane when I only live three blocks from the coast. Actually, in Mississippi, we hardly ever evacuate because there is no need to. We are higher than New Orleans. Hurricane Camille was the worst hurricane of all and it only put five inches of water in my house. Every other hurricane had only put water in the yard.

Not only do my house and my mother's house sit a little higher than most of the other homes in our area, but they were also built well. I knew they were strong houses. But from what Hurricane Katrina delivered, I don't know how they survived. It is hard to imagine the amount of water that came through here, to envision what happened.

What you need to consider when deciding to evacuate or not is how high your home is above sea level. My house sits about eighteen to twenty feet above sea level, so we felt safe staying here. Besides, we went through Hurricane Camille and we were safe. A lot of people thought the same thing would be true about Katrina. We all thought that we would be safe.

They say that Camille killed more people in 2005 than she did in 1969. That was due to the thinking that since they survived Camille, they would be fine during Katrina. This thinking resulted in many deaths during Katrina. Everyone thought that nothing could top Camille. Mother Nature had different plans!

There are other reasons why people stayed and did not leave. One, by the time people get boarded up, it's too late to leave. Plus, it's expensive to leave. It takes a lot of money. You have to have a place to go to, like a hotel. You need money for gas, for food, etc.

In July, right before Hurricane Katrina hit, people down here had evacuated for Hurricane Cindy. She did not hit us, but everyone left. Nothing happened, so people came home. The year before, a similar thing happened with Hurricane Ivan. Everybody left, but nothing happened. It did not hit. Some people had the attitude that they were not going to leave because they figured it was not going to hit us. That was a second reason.

Typically, since Louisiana sticks out and is so low, people there get evacuated first. However, due to Lake Pontchartrain, people from New Orleans cannot evacuate directly to the north. So, they need to either go east or west in order to go north. That means some people from Louisiana have to come into Mississippi and catch Interstate 55 or 59 north. Mississippi residents need to wait and give the interstates to those coming from New Orleans, because of the situation that they are in. All the highways are changed to traffic going only north. This is called contra flow. All the southbound lanes are now headed north, until they get to Hattiesburg, Mississippi. At Hattiesburg, the highway splits in several different directions and the traffic is directed into those highways.

So, to evacuate, they start at coastal Louisiana and move back. At some point, when Mississippi residents are instructed to leave, Interstate 10 is blocked. In other words, Louisiana traffic can no longer come to 10. It has to go north. Mississippi traffic goes to 10 and then heads to Mobile, Alabama, to take Interstate 65 north, or continues east to Florida.

All this is necessary because there are about two million people who have to get out in a short period of time. This is not something that can be done very quickly. So, the states have to communicate. For example, Shreveport, Louisiana, is about a five-hour drive by car. However, during a hurricane evacuation it could take eighteen hours. A lot of people run out of gas on the side of the highway. But, we are learning. The federal government has sent down gas trucks to help people stranded on the side of the highway because their fuel tanks are empty. This helps to keep people moving.

Anyway, we were told that this would not be as bad as Camille. No one could imagine another hurricane as bad as Camille. So, many people stayed for Katrina, and it *did* hit us. Katrina came in at thirty-one feet! Had I known that, I certainly would have left. The bottom line is, every storm is different and you just do not know.

Prelude to a Storm

On Saturday, we knew Katrina was coming but it was just a category two storm. That is nothing to worry about. Katrina was supposed to turn and go up the coast of Florida around Appalachia University in Tallahassee, Florida. Well, it kept drifting. Then they said it was going to go into Pensacola Florida, and then it was here. The thinking was it would come into western Louisiana (like where hurricane Rita hit in Sept. of 2005). If that were the case, it would be no problem for us.

However, with the drifting it ended up turning south and picked up more steam over a hot pocket in the gulf.

There were no big hurricanes that season in the Gulf of Mexico before Katrina. There was a little bitty one named Cindy that hit Florida, but it was not enough to churn up the Gulf, to take the cold waters and send them up. Actually, the Gulf of Mexico was baking when Katrina came across. When Katrina hit that hot pocket, it exploded!

That Saturday night I had been to a fiftieth wedding anniversary party. Everyone left a little early, because of the storm. Although it was just a category two, I said I would keep an eye on it. My daughter, who attends Mississippi State, was in town that night. I told her she needed to get up early Sunday morning in case they called for an evacuation so that she could beat the traffic and get back to school on time, as she had about a five-hour drive.

About five o'clock I got up and turned on the TV. Katrina had gone from a category two to a category five overnight. That was unheard of! It went from 115 mph winds to 170 mph winds! It became a massive hurricane all because of that hot pocket and she started turning north.

By six o'clock Sunday morning, they knew it was coming to the northern gulf, no question about it. Preparations for a category four or five hurricane are totally different than for a category one, two or three. For a category three, which is a pretty good-sized hurricane, we would board up my two front windows, and get my lawn furniture in. For category five, we board up all the windows, and take out everything of value, because you just do not know how bad it will be. We thought this was not going to be a Camille, but it was going to be bad.

Camille was a little tiny storm that had been packed tightly. She was not very big across. Camille is what they call a Mississippi hurricane; because when she came in, she just hit the Mississippi coast. Katrina hit from Louisiana all the way to Florida. Camille was tiny, but compact. Camille brought in a twenty-four foot tidal surge that was unheard of. Most tidal surges were about twelve to fifteen feet prior to that. Katrina's surge was thirty-one feet!

Camille was the only storm that had ever flooded *this* yard. She put five to eight inches in the house. The water went up and forty-five minutes later, it went down. When Camille came in, our plan was to close the iron gates to keep the trash out, but let the water come through. Then, we could just hose it down afterward. We thought we could follow the same plan with Katrina. However, the problem with Katrina was we ended up with six inches on the *second* floor. That kind of messed up the plan.

Camille had 223 mph winds. That was not the gusts. That was wind! A gust was clocked at 240 mph. In Gulfport, the winds pushed three ships onto land. They had to be cut up. Everyone was thinking Camille, Camille. That was the storm, Camille.

Now we were told Katrina was going to be bad. By the time everything got boarded up and secured, it was late Sunday evening. The storm is coming in Sunday night or Monday morning. Where are you going to go? Traffic is crazy on the interstate. The problem we have here is figuring out where the storm is going. Is it moving this way or that way? For example, if it is coming from Florida, you want to go west. At this time, it was still uncertain exactly where she was coming in.

Part of the problem with Katrina is it was coming in with 175 mph winds. The prediction was the that winds would be 125 mph to 135 mph when it hit the coast. How much water will come in is based on the speed of the wind. There are charts designed to help you predict the speed of the wind and the amount of water that would come in accordingly. With winds at 125 mph, we should have had a fifteen to eighteen foot tidal surge.

What was not realized at the time was the amount of tidal surge for 175 mph winds. The winds start to die down as the water becomes shallower. It loses its energy source. However, the water is not going to disappear from the surge created by those 175 mph winds. They misjudged Katrina.

I tell people that I am not stupid. I am at an elevation of twenty feet. If I had been told there was going to be a storm surge of thirty feet, I am going to leave! However, if you tell me the surge will be eighteen feet and I am at an elevation of twenty feet, I can handle two feet of water. That is fine. At least I will be here and I can pick stuff up and see what's going on, just like Camille.

My younger daughter wanted to stay down here with me. She had never really been through a hurricane. I said that that would be no problem. The year before, when hurricane Ivan was coming, we got ready for it, but he hit Florida. So, we didn't really have a whole lot.

We got everything ready, and everything boarded up. You eat real good before a hurricane. It is kind of like a party; well, not really a party, but you eat good. That is because you never know when you might get a chance to eat good again. You could end up with no electricity. People bring stuff, including candy, to pass the time. We ate steaks and baked potatoes.

My sister brought a ham. I told her that I would bake it so that we would have it for sandwiches for after the storm in case we lost our electricity.

Everything was going according to plan. By about four o'clock Sunday evening, there was nothing left to do. It is really the most boring thing when there is nothing left to do and you are just waiting for the hurricane to come. You watch the TV waiting for the next hurricane report, which comes out once every three hours. If it comes out at one o'clock, every TV station is giving you the same information. That is the only thing they can broadcast, like what the coordinates are, what they expect, etc. So, you sit there and listen to the same story on every channel.

I could tell that my daughter was getting bored. We had just finished boarding up the front windows, and she took a picture of it. Kidding around, I commented, "Come on! Let's go take some before and after pictures." She got in the truck and we went down by the water to take pictures. We never even thought that it was possible that there would soon be nothing left.

Rescue

as told by Mike Kovacevich

Watching and Waiting

In my house at this time were me and my daughter, my mom, my little nephew, my sister Beverly and her fiancé, as well as Chucky and Fletcher Fest and their mama, Miss Winnie. They lived behind us in a low area, so they always came to stay with us. Everything was going pretty good. Everyone had eaten. I took the ham out of the oven about ten o'clock Sunday evening and I set it on the counter to cool on a big pan that I had. Then I decided to go lay down since the storm wasn't supposed to hit until the next morning. I had been up all day and decided to get some sleep.

While everyone else was watching a movie downstairs, I went upstairs. I had my sister's cat upstairs with me. All totaled, we had five dogs in the house. Since the dogs stayed downstairs, I took the cat up with me. I lay down until about two-thirty in the morning when I woke up. I went downstairs to find everyone still watching TV. They were just waiting. That is all you could do, just wait.

I walked out onto the porch. The street was underwater at the corner, which is normal, if we have had a lot of rain. This was the rain that came in from the feeder bands before the hurricane hits. These are the clouds that come in ahead of it. It can be very calm when all of a sudden, boom! It starts pouring down rain, and it is windy. Then ten minutes later, it is calm again. The spinning causes the clouds and the gusts of wind to come through. The others said it had been raining for a bit.

I asked them if it had been pouring down raining. Well, they said that it had been raining, but not pouring. I walked around to another side of the house to check another street. When it rains, if this front street was under water, then that other street should have been under water. No water. The other street had no water.

A limb had fallen out of an oak tree. I got it and stuck it in neutral ground. Joey, Beverly's fiancé, came out and said, "What's wrong?"

I replied, "That's seawater!"

He said, "No, it ain't!"

I said, "Watch that stick." We sat out there and you could see the water steadily creeping up to the stick. "That's not good."

Hurricane George had hit us in 1998, and put water up to the edge of the grass, which was a pretty good-sized surge. Even though I saw the water creeping up, I still thought that we would be okay. I did holler at the Vietnamese family who lived on the corner with two little girls about ten and twelve years old that they needed to get out.

He said, "No, we'll be all right. We'll be all right."

We continued to watch the water. About four o'clock Monday morning, it started getting pretty deep. We noticed that the water was coming from the east, which was from the bay, not from the beach.

We walked across the street to look behind that house and noticed that there was water coming from the beach as well. The water was coming from those two directions, the beach and the bay, and it met at the other side of my mom's driveway.

At this time, about four-thirty, there was water in the driveway, but not in my yard yet. I yelled at the Vietnamese man and said that I was coming to get the kids. He asked where they were going. I told him that I was bringing them into my house.

I waded over in water about waist deep. I picked up the first little girl—I grabbed her and carried her over here—and I gave her to Joey. Then, I went and got the other little girl. The man said that he needed to get some stuff. Then I went and got him and his wife, and they brought some suitcases over. He was worried about his car. His car was parked along the street on a slant. I told him not to worry about his car. It would be all right.

Across the street, I noticed that a young man named Jeremy kept opening his door and looking out, opening the door and looking out. He kept checking like he was expecting water to come in their home. I called his father, who was at a house down the street and told him that we were fixing to go get Jeremy. His father said that he would call Jeremy and let him know. As we went across the street, the water at the end of the driveway was quite deep due to a dip in the road. But, we got Jeremy and brought him back over to our house and gave him a steak, which he ate.

Now it is about five-thirty and the lights went off. I am thinking to myself that we had done good. We only had about thirty minutes yet until daylight. We made it through the worst part of the night and soon we would be able to see.

When daylight broke, as far as you could see there was nothing but water. The water was moving down the street. Although the cars were still above water in my driveway, we could not drive them anywhere. So I thought to myself, "Okay, now what do we do?"

I could see that I still had no water in my yard yet, but I knew my mom was about to get water because it was already creeping up in her yard. I decided that we should go over to my mom's house and remove all the stuff we had left there from the floor. We went over and stacked the sofa on the table in order to make things higher. We had already brought my mother's valuables and important things to my house, but had left the kitchen table and the sofas and things like that—things that could be more easily replaced.

Although I had nailed her French doors shut, and had metal on the outside to help hold them fast, the wind was hitting so hard that the metal was starting to bend. The doors were trying to blow. At that point, I said that we needed to go.

The last thing I did was to grab her big TV. I carried it to the top of the stairs and set it on the floor. Well, that TV ended up floating off! We also moved the cars in her yard over to my yard because it was a little bit higher.

Somewhere in the neighborhood of about eight o'clock, water got in her house. We were not worried about it because she had marble floors and paneling on the walls, which could be replaced.

Around eight-thirty there was a guy over on the side of the street that started hollering out his window that they had water. I also had water in my yard at this time. It had come up to the second step of my porch and seemed to have quit rising, but in his house it was getting deep. He was screaming out the window. He had a handicapped wife, who was an older lady, and he was trying to get her into the attic but he couldn't.

So, we went out the back door into chest high water and made it to the fence. We had to lift her over the fence. It was me, my little nephew Debryan, Joey, Jeremy, and Chuckie. The neighbors also had a dog with them, but he was in a cage. (He was a mean little Chihuahua.) As we got the lady over the fence, and I was carrying her into the house, you could feel the debris under the water, like pieces of wood, hitting against your legs. It took us quite a while to get there and back. Then the people next door started hollering.

There were seven in that house. They were going to get in the attic. We went and got them out, too. We slowly walked through more chest high water to get to them. By now the water was higher than the chain-link fence. So first, we had to find where the fence was in order to get them over it.

Some of the people we had to actually kind of hold over our heads because the water was so deep and walked them back to the house. You could not swim in the water because the wind was blowing, the current was strong and it was filled with debris. You had to walk very slowly. If you tried to go out into water that was over your head and swim, you ended up going in a different direction than what you wanted. The 145 mph wind moved the water in the direction it was blowing.

Meanwhile, everybody's in the house looking out at the water, which is about five feet deep. Water as far as you could see. However, I still did not have water in my house and the water stopped rising. The wind continued blowing like crazy. We watched a house roof blow off. We watched things go floating by.

Then my brother called, a little after nine. He asked me if we had water yet. I told him that it was just coming in now and that I would call him back. The water was pushing in through the drains and overflowing on the floor, just like it did during Camille. We started picking up stuff. I'm thinking that if it's like Camille, we will only get five inches. So, we put the sofa up on top of the coffee table. Things like that.

Everything that we had brought from my mom's house, we had boxed. It was sitting on my dining room floor. There were so many people in my house that we had an assembly line sending all of her things up the stairs. My stuff, we just picked up.

The water continued to rise. My brother called me back and asked where the water was now. I told him that it had done passed Camille. I said that it could not get any higher. He said, "Yes, it can!" I asked him to let me go so that I could finish picking up stuff. I told him that I would call him back.

I realized that the storm was probably at its peak. As I looked out the back door at the rising water, I saw what looked like Jesus hanging on the cross. The wind had pressed a white cloth against a cross-shaped tree. It looked just like a crucifix. I felt like someone was looking over us.

Surviving the Storm

I continued to pick things up off the floor. I had every window boarded up so I could not see outside. The front door offered the only view. As I set something on top of the stereo, I glanced out the front door. I was standing in four inches of water around my ankles, but when I looked out the window, the water was over my head on the other side of that door! I thought, "Oh-oh!" and yelled, "Everybody upstairs!" I knew that if the door blew open and the water rushed through there, it would knock the walls and everything else out.

Believe it or not, it took a little over an hour for the water inside to catch up with the water outside. The door did not burst open. The windows did not crash in. The water just seeped in. We could see little bubbles where the water was seeping through the floor.

We all went upstairs. I thought about calling my brother back, but you could not just call somebody because the service was not there. Besides that, I did not have a clue where my phone was. Then someone said, "Your phone!" I heard it ringing and found it. It was my brother calling me back.

He said, "Hey man, how's it going?"

I said, "It's going alright." Now I'm upstairs and I've got my sister, my nephew, my daughter, my mama, and all our family and friends. There were twenty-three of us up there with six dogs, a cat and a parrot. Upstairs there were only two bedrooms and a foyer. That is it. Everyone is packed in, and it is very hot.

The storm really affected the animals. They were in shock. Even today, if neighborhood kids pop firecrackers for the Fourth of July, or if there is a thunderstorm, we have to give my dog medicine to help keep her calm. She still remembers Katrina!

My brother said, "Where's the water?" I was trying to be calm about it. I told him that the water was above the last window. He continued, "That ain't too bad." I repeated to him that it was *above* the last window. He asked, "What are you trying to tell me?" I told him that the water was touching the chandeliers. He went ballistic! I ended up trying to calm him down. I told him to calm down, because we were okay.

Originally, my little brother and his wife were supposed to come stay with us as well. She was pregnant, due in November. At the last minute they decided to go stay with her brother in North Jackson County. It was a good thing that she was not here. He kept calling me.

My other little brother in D'Iberville kept calling too. They knew that we had water, but they had no clue how much water we had. The last they had heard, it was up to the light switches. He called and said, "Hey, you're going to get the eye. It should be in about twenty or thirty minutes." I was glad to hear that.

One of the guys we had rescued asked why we wanted the eye, because that was the worst part. I told him it was because we needed the wind to quit blowing. Because every time the wind blew, it created waves. You could look out and see a wave hit a house. By the third wave, that house collapsed. The waves were like bulldozers hitting the houses. We really needed the wind to quit blowing.

Well, we never actually saw the eye. In reality, we *were* in the worst part. The winds around the eye are the strongest, but the winds east of the eye are the worst. That's where we were. You do not get relief. It is steady winds. Later, my brother called and said that we were not getting the eye. I told him that I had already figured that out!

Then we lost contact. I could pick up my cell phone and call long distances, like to Chicago, but I could not call across the street. My oldest daughter, who had returned to college at Mississippi State was freaking out. The last I had spoken with her was about three that morning. She asked me to be honest with her. So I was.

At that point, I told her the water was just in the street and that we were high and we would be fine. I told her not to worry about us, that we would be fine. She asked if I was sure we would be all right, and I told her we would be.

Later, the only person she could get in touch with was my brother in North Jackson County. He is relaying messages back and forth. At this point, the water is high and they know that it is bad. He's telling my daughter what's going on and he is freaking out. He does not want his wife to see how upset he is so he's outside in the carport talking and crying. He is telling my daughter that it looks bad. She cannot get in touch with us. Nobody could get in touch with us. We had lost communication with everybody. At this point, there ain't nothing to do but wait. Wait and pray.

We waited upstairs. The water kept coming up. About eleven o'clock, a girl around the corner called and said, "Come get me!" It was her, her mother, and three little girls. I told her that I would not be able to come get her right now, because I had seven feet of water in my living room. She told me that she had called someone and was advised to get on the roof.

I said, "Listen to me. Do *not* get on that roof!"

She said, "But they said…"

I told her, "I don't care what they told you! Do not get on the roof. I've been gauging the water and the water has quit rising." For some reason, and I don't know why, we had a yardstick sitting at the top of the stairs. We could gauge the level of the water out of the upstairs window, by comparing the water level to the window. We knew when it had stopped rising.

I repeated, "It has stopped rising. Stay where you are and I will come get you when the water gets low enough." She asked me if I was sure about all this and I told her that I was. I repeated to her that she should not get on that roof.

Even though the water had stopped rising, the winds were still very strong. We were still in the middle of the storm. The winds were about 145 mph and they were constant, not just puffs. It was coming at you and it would not let up.

That's what gets me when people say there were no winds in the storm, that it was just water. There was a lot of wind in this storm. Not only did the wind blow the trees over, but it blew the leaves right off the trees. The next day there was still a lot of wind. It blew, and it blew and it blew.

So here we were. Camille was tiny compared to Katrina and we were on the wrong end of Katrina. We had to wait for Katrina to get all the way past us before the winds could blow the water out. That did not happen until about five o'clock in the evening. So there we sat with a house full of water.

View from the Top

The good thing was, nobody panicked, nobody started crying and crying. Well, my daughter cried for about a minute because my sister Beverly had started crying when she looked out the window and saw all the debris coming in between the two houses. You could hear the debris outside hitting the house—bam, bam, bam! On the inside, you could hear the furniture floating around and crashing into the walls. You could hear the clinking as it hit the chandeliers. Every time it hit the chandeliers, my sister would lose it. What were you going to do?

I had this antique china cabinet filled with knickknacks and other antiques. It was made of two pieces. When the water got deep enough, the top piece floated off, and as it fell, you could hear everything inside it crashing. Everybody just looked. You could see in their eyes what they were thinking, but no one said anything. Everybody kept quiet.

When we first went upstairs, we were all in such a rush that no one thought to bring any food or water with them. As we continued to watch and wait upstairs, we saw the ham on a platter go floating out the back door. Everybody was yelling, "There's the ham!" They were all hungry. I was starving. None of us had anything to eat since the evening before.

I thought that my little nephew was going to cry. He yelled, "There's the ham!"

I said, "Yep, there goes the ham."

Before the storm, I had also made some garlic mashed potatoes. They came floating out behind the ham. My daughter shouts, "There go the potatoes!" I also had a big pot of green beans on the stove.

Now, the potatoes and green beans were in two separate pots, both on the stove. Remember, there was seven feet of water in the house. The potatoes floated off. But the green beans were still on the stove when I left the house after the water went down. They did not move one inch. How does that happen? It just does not make sense.

As we looked down on the watery world from upstairs, we saw many strange things. We watched my mom's roof blow off her house. The walls of my mother's cement garage collapsed. We could see none of the vehicles that we had parked by the garage. All six cars were totally underwater.

We saw the floating docks from the casino, Isle of Capri, hundreds of them, racing by. We saw a piece of the boardwalk from the beach go by. There was a little tree between my house and my mother's, which caught a lot of this debris. We saw a TV float around the house, twice!

We watched as buildings went completely underwater. We saw houses floating down the street as though they were houseboats on the river. In one spot, the house that sat there in the morning floated away, and another house floated into its spot by the end of the day.

At this point, you don't know what the next step is. We tried to stay one step ahead of the storm. We were prepared. The water came in, and we went upstairs. Now what happens? Where do we go from here? My mom is elderly, Miss Winnie is elderly, and you start to think that you cannot save everybody, so who do you save? I got my daughter, my sister, my nephew, and my mom.

And then I started thinking about if we decided to go out in the water. Where would we go? Do we go to a particular house? There was no way to keep everybody together. I was thinking about maybe trying to get to the big old live oak tree.

Then, here comes a house. We were watching this house coming right at us. I'm thinking that this house is fixing to hit us, and it's going to really mess us up, because it's going to knock us off the foundation. But, the big oak tree beside my house stopped that floating house dead. It wedged that house and stopped it cold. In doing so, this ancient live oak tree, that was about eight feet across, split in half.

I knew that if that house had hit us it would cause a big problem, because before I went upstairs, I realized that someone's living room floor had hit one of the porch columns and took it out. There was only one column holding up the porch. If that house had hit us, the porch would have fallen and we would have been totally exposed upstairs. We would have been out in the elements.

At the time, I was the only one that knew this because I stayed down in the water until it was about chest high. I kept thinking to myself that this could not be good. I was concerned the porch roof was going to fall. We had no choice. We had to go upstairs. The only thing that saved us was that the water got so high, that it kept the roof floating and the roof could not fall.

Although we had wind, the main thing was the water. It came up and it just did not want to go down. We could not figure out why the water wouldn't go out. We had seven feet of water inside this house for eight hours, and I'm at twenty feet. What we did not realize at the time was that before Katrina hit land, it had just exploded and its size was tremendous. Not only that, it had a double eye wall, which made it worse. Everything that could possibly go wrong went wrong.

The scariest part was being upstairs in my house for seven or eight hours with the water as high as it could go, looking out, and knowing that you were the only thing left above water. Everything else was gone.

The Worst to Come

My little brother called and said that the water was fixing to go down as the winds were shifting. He said that we would be all right. I told him that the worst was yet to come. He asked me why I said that. I told him to think about that. I said that all this water had come in over a long period of time. However, it is about to quickly go out at one time.

The strong winds and rain were sucking everything back out to the gulf. A hurricane is like a big top spinning. As it comes in, it's pushing all the water into the land. However, when the wind spins around to the back side, it pushes all the water back to the gulf. It takes everything back to the gulf with it, even some people's houses.

Suddenly, there was a sound like that of a cannon going off. The windows downstairs were blown out. When I looked downstairs to see what the noise was, a statue of the Blessed Virgin Mary was looking through the window at me. Although the wind was sucking every piece of the furniture right out of the house, she stayed right there, even with the strong current.

As the water started to recede, much quicker than it came in, we were able to go downstairs and check out our situation. I told the guys that no women and children should go down just yet, as we weren't sure what we would find. Only the guys went down in order to figure out a way to get out of this house.

As we eased down the stairs, we watched as the furniture swirled around. We grabbed what furniture we could and floated it to the side. The TV in the corner of my front room ended up at the back of the house. The TV in the back ended up in the front. Those little bitty things just did not make sense.

I gazed outside and knew that I could not get out of my house until I got the debris off the porch. In some spots, it was piled up about five feet deep. As a matter of fact, when we finally got the porch cleared there was a street sign on my front steps. It was from Oak and Eighth Street, which was eight blocks north.

What was so amazing was with all that strong current, the house did not move. As we looked out over the neighborhood, there were blocks and blocks of nothing but just rubbled houses. I told the guys that we needed to bust into houses to look for canned goods. The husband of the handicapped woman said that he had plenty of canned goods. I said, "No, you don't."

He insisted that he had just stocked up. I told him again that he did not have any canned goods. He said, "No, really! I have plenty!" Finally, he squeezed through a wall and bent down to take a look outside around the rubble. I pointed at his house, and he realized that he did not have a house. The water had taken his whole house. The only thing that was left, was his roof lying on top of his car.

As the water continued to go down, we realized that there were actually two people in the house that had wedged in my tree. I knew whose house it was because I recognized the siding. This house had floated from about a block away. The house next door to their house had hit them and knocked them off their foundation. When I realized they were still in the house we went to get them. We balanced ourselves on the wall of the wreckage to get them.

When I got there, I needed to remove a piece of paneling that the young man had placed at an opening to try to block the wind. There was very little of the house remaining to hold them up. When I looked down beyond the small six-foot span that was supporting them, I saw the car that belonged to the Vietnamese man. That is the man who I had told earlier his car would be okay.

The city of Biloxi has a tape of a 911 call placed by the young man in this house. As it happened, the 911 receiver was a friend of the young man's. On the tape, he was recorded calling out the operator's name and screaming that he and Mama were going to die, because mama could not swim. The 911 operator was working to try to calm him down.

As they floated along, they had no idea that there was no first or second story underneath them. They were trapped in the tiny attic room that remained. That is where they stayed for about eight hours until we got them out.

Then, I remembered the girl with the three young children and her mother who had called asking for help earlier. I waded over there to get them. I had to go out the back, around the shed, over a fence, and through a guy's house to get to them. I brought them back to my house the same way, just in reverse.

After the water finally emptied out of the house, and we knew it was okay, everyone moved onto the porch. There were now thirty people on my porch waiting for someone to find them. We had begun the night before with nine people in the house and had pulled twenty-one people from the waters. There was still water in the yard and in the street. We had no idea where we were going to go.

I waded down to the fire station. I asked about somebody getting all the people from my house. They responded that they were waiting for someone to come get them! The firemen had been left behind at the station. When it was time for them to leave with the fire truck, the water was too deep. They had spent the day on top of the fire truck with water over their knees.

Then we saw some people in trees across the street waving to us. They had stayed in their home, but when it went under water, they climbed onto the roof. Since the water kept coming, they climbed into the trees. They were stuck in the trees since the water was too deep for them to climb down yet.

Later, when the water was going out, firemen did go to help the people stuck in the trees to get down. Unfortunately, there were other people from the neighborhood in the trees as well, but they did not make it. Sadly, they drowned.

Moving Forward
as told by Mike Kovacevich

Hopeful Beginnings

The storm ended around five o'clock. As soon as possible after the winds had shifted and the water started going out, the city sent bulldozers down the street. That opened up the street for my family to find us as well. The National Guard came down the street, but I told them to keep on going because nobody was hurt here. By six-thirty that evening, my family arrived to take us away.

I have two brothers and a sister that live on a big piece of property in D'Iberville. They came and got us, and took us out there. There were about fifty of us that piled in there that night. Here, they mostly had wind damage. So we were able to hook up some generators to their refrigerators to help keep food cold. I stayed there until November of 2008, little over three years. I slept on my sister's floor.

When we were being picked up to go back to my sister's house, I remember a sight that stuck with me. We saw a family walking down the street. The little boy had no shoes on his feet. My nephew, who was nine years old at the time, took off his shoes and gave them to the little barefoot boy. They had lost everything they owned. They had nothing but the clothes they had on, and the clothes they had on were soaking wet. The really sad thing was they didn't know where they were going. Their home was gone, and the shelters went down. They were just walking, trying to find a place to go. It was a rough situation.

That first night after the storm, although my family members went to my sister's house with me, some of the people we had rescued stayed at my house up on the second floor. That was helpful to me as well, because then the house would be secured. The very next day, there were people going through neighborhoods and looting people's houses.

Right after the storm, we did have ways of getting food. The Red Cross and the Salvation Army came in and brought food for us. My favorite was Papa John's Pizza. They came in with a pizza kitchen, cooked 100,000 little pizzas, and just handed them out to people. So, we had food, but we couldn't just go to a grocery store and buy groceries. They had all been underwater.

Also, there were no telephones to call each other. The police could not talk to each other, because all the towers were down. The hospitals were down. To get to a hospital was almost impossible because all the roads were clogged with debris and houses. Many people came out of their houses with only the clothing they had on. For three days, it was pretty bad. It was a chaotic situation.

To deal with the debris, the city dug big holes the size of football fields and pushed the debris into them. When they finished, it was determined that some of these holes were forty-seven football fields high. In other words, they were like a three-story building. Then they put dirt over it. Over the years, the debris will decay and the mound will fall.

Next, they gathered up all the trees that had fallen down. Again, a big hole was dug for all the trees. They started burning trees on September 11, 2005. The fire did not go out until July of 2006 because they were still bringing in trees felled by Katrina. That fire even continued to burn during hurricane Rita, which arrived about a month after Katrina. Even hurricane Rita did not put out that fire.

My daughter had taken lots of pictures as things progressed to help her get through the storm. She had just started on the annual staff at school. She had only been in school for about two weeks and had her camera handy. She took pictures of the debris, of things in the house as they floated around, what she saw in the backyard, and all around the house.

There were many amazing things that happened. In my bedroom, I had a crucifix hanging on the wall. You could see a watermark right at Christ's head. His head, however, did not go under the water. Another incredible thing after the storm was the statues that many people had in their yards. All the statues were still standing—all of them. Now, at St. Michael's, the big Catholic Church, all the statues fell except the Blessed Virgin Mary. She was still hanging on the wall.

I tried to find the rightful owner of the statue of the Blessed Virgin Mary that ended up on our porch. It did not belong to St. Michael's. No one else claimed it, so the priest told me to keep it on the porch. He said that's where she belonged. The statue has been there ever since.

We knew that during the storm there were a lot of prayers for us. Evidently, somebody upstairs was looking over us. When you realize that five hundred houses disappeared, and yours is the only one left standing with thirty people—you never know. We were fortunate that we did not lose anyone in my family.

However, I did know some people that perished during the storm. I know of twelve people in my neighborhood that drowned. There are still people who are unaccounted and unidentified from the storm. There is not a real number on how many people died during Katrina. Part of that reason has to do with tourists.

Biloxi is a tourist town. There were no records to tell us exactly who was in town that night. People from up North, or other visitors, would not know exactly how to respond in the event of a hurricane. Some of them ended up drowned or washed out into the gulf. No one knows for sure.

I'm also thankful that the old oak tree that prevented the floating house from crashing into my home is healing. Although the tree stopped the home, it suffered a major split in its trunk. It is amazing that it did not fall down. Although this split has seemed to heal, there are still some major gaps. I'm thinking about putting some bolts through it to help to strengthen it.

My sixty-year-old pecan tree also managed to survive. It has the best pecans with paper shells. Everybody wants these pecans. They are good! Some things endured.

Rebuilding Struggles

Old Biloxi families, living in homes one hundred years old with fancy woodwork, had owned all of this area around my house. It was a nice neighborhood. Katrina cleaned it out. There were five hundred houses around here that disappeared. When the water went down, the only two houses left standing in this part of Old Biloxi were my mother's home and the home I live in, which had been my grandparents. Everything looks so empty. One other family has rebuilt, but that is it.

Part of the reason more people have not rebuilt has to do with insurance. The federal government has raised the flood level from thirteen feet to twenty-two feet since Katrina. This means you would have to build your house way up in the air to get it that high. Yet if you did that, insurance won't cover you. So, there is nothing really being built in this area. Wind, hail, and fire insurance for your home used to cost about $2200 a year before the storm. Now, insurance could be up to $4000 a year just for wind only. Nobody can afford it.

Many of these people have packed up and moved north of Interstate 10 in order to get away from the tidal surges. Communities north of Interstate 10 are booming.

Even businesses cannot afford it. The business district in Biloxi runs down Highway 90, Beach Boulevard, and there is a lot of empty space. The businesses that would like to rebuild can't, because they cannot afford the insurance. At first, there was talk of building many condos and high rises along the coast. However, that fell through due to the economy. I would estimate it will take about fifteen years before everything comes back to normal.

We do have casinos that help the economy. During Katrina, the casinos were what we call "dockside." This means that they had to be on the water, and they had to float. That was what the zoning required. When the storm came in, the water got so high that they all floated off—all twelve of them! Some of these casinos were three story buildings, three football fields long.

The casino industry had decided that they were not coming back because this could happen again. So, the local government decided to let them come and build on land, eight hundred feet from where they were. This has been really helpful because a lot of people work in the casino industry.

A number of the casinos even paid their employees for one year after the hurricane, even though they were not working, in order to get back on their feet. Some casinos even brought their employees in for classes on how to install sheet rock, on how to do electrical work, etc., so that they could go out and find a job until the casinos were ready to reopen. The only real boost here in Biloxi has been the casinos reopening to get people back to work to bring in the tourists to increase the tax dollars.

Several months after the storm, my mom was getting depressed. She wanted to be home. We had her in a little FEMA cottage. We kept promising her she would be home, but we kept having delays. Then, we got connected with RAI, a recovery organization.

With help from volunteers, we did everything we could and got her in her house before Thanksgiving of 2008. I actually moved in her house a week before she did to get everything ready. We hung pictures on the wall for her. Everything was fixed up. The first thing we had in my mom's newly renovated house was a birthday party for my little niece who was born in November right after the storm. Then we all celebrated Thanksgiving here, which had been our family tradition.

In 2008, it was a lot different down here than it is now. There were lots of homeless people. I came down here with my mom to let people know that someone was living here.

Now, there aren't as many people. I am still working on getting my house finished.

It was more urgent for my mom to get back in her home, as she is eighty-one years old. She's like a new person now. She fell and broke her hip last year, but she is doing fine now. She is running all over the place. My niece was getting married in Wyoming, and I had wanted my mother to go to the wedding. She said that she didn't want to, because it was too cold and she would probably slip and fall on the ice. Instead, she stayed home and tripped over a cement block at a ballgame and broke her hip.

Although I am still working on my home, it's not in bad shape. The house stayed firm on its foundation during the storm. The floors did not even buckle. At the time, the people who had stayed in my home during the storm were making fun of me, because I insisted that they keep sweeping the water out of the house as it receded.

When the water was down to about four inches, I asked them to start sweeping the floor. They would sweep a little, and then watch the water roll back in. I told them to just keep sweeping. They said that they pushed it out and it just came back in. They insisted that it was not working. I told them that they did not understand.

What they did not realize, was that by us keeping the water moving, we did not allow the mud to settle. So, I had very little mud on this floor. Although I was only ten years old during hurricane Camille, I remember all the mud that we had to clean out then. I thought it was worth a try to keep sweeping and keep the mud out.

One thing I did have to do was put on a new back door. It had gotten blown out. However, that was probably one of the best things that happened for us. Since the door blew out, the water was able to keep right on moving through. Here in the kitchen, I still have the original windows from when the house was built in 1948. During the storm, you could barely hear the wind blowing through because these windows are so secure.

I still have the original cabinets. I just refinished them. The cabinets were actually made out of the same tongue and groove that was used for the wood floor. When I bought this house, I removed the wall between the kitchen and the dining room to open it up. I have a friend who bought some pecan wood and used that to make cabinets for under the bar that was built where the wall had been removed.

When you have a family my size over, you need a lot of room. At Thanksgiving, we often have at least sixty-five people. We put the kids all in the back room. The adults are mostly in the dining room. We have a big circle of food that you follow to fill your plate. I'm hoping to have Thanksgiving here at my home again in 2010.

Connections

Through RAI and the people that have come to work on my mom's house, we have met the most wonderful people— so many good people. We have met people from all over the world. They have come from India, Australia, Germany, England, etc. We have had kids and adults alike. I keep a list of everyone who has come. We have tried to keep in touch with everyone who has come to help. We send out Christmas cards to people and to various churches. Some of them come back and give us a call once in a while.

For example, we had a group of high school kids that came to us from San Francisco. They were wonderful. They were a blast! We got to be really close with them. Some of the girls call me constantly. They want to come back down. Some of them are in college now.

Another group from St. Olaf's College does the same thing. They call and keep in touch. They want to know what is going on.

Another time we met a group of high school students that had come from Boston. I shared with them that I was going to go to Boston the following year with some of my family. I explained that we were going to watch the Yankees play against the Red Sox. I added that I had never been there, so they told me all about the area.

In July of 2009, when my nephew was playing baseball for Southern Miss, the team went to the College World Series for the first time ever. He got invited to play in the Cape Cod League. He made the Cape Cod All-Star game, which was played in Fenway Park. So, again, about twelve other family members and I went up to Boston for the game.

As I had been to Boston before and knew a little bit about how to get around, I could show my daughters and other relatives the sites such as Paul Revere's house. We were walking down the streets of downtown Boston for a walking tour. I'm leading the group and walking ahead of them so that they would follow me. If I did not do that, I would never get them moving again when they got to a stop sign.

I stayed about a block ahead of them to keep them moving. We had to be at the docks by four o'clock to go on a whale watching tour. We only had so much time to do the things on our list and get to the boat.

As I'm walking down the busy streets of Boston, a group of people came up behind me. As they passed me one of the guys stopped to look at me. I overheard him tell a girl that he knew me, that I was from Biloxi, Mississippi. They all stopped and questioned him. He said, "Yes, I know that guy! That's Mike! We worked on his house." They could not get over it. What were the odds of that?

I tell everyone that the biggest story was the storm, but the second biggest story was the volunteers. Yes, we have met some great people from all across the country. We have met some incredible people. Everyone is so friendly. There are really no words to describe it. The work they do is incredible. If the volunteers did not come we would be in bad shape. Things will never be the same. But, with the help of new friends, we are still here.

"Beginning Again"

Katrina created tenacity	Grit
Determination	Ambitions
Removed obstacles	Removed obstacles
Generated motivation	Opportunity for accomplishments
Fostered self-discipline	Encouraged persistence
Having task commitment	Having task commitment
Finding your passion	Make it your life's work
Accept constructive criticism	Here, see, and accept optimism
Praises for efforts	Praises for efforts
Failure on different levels is inevitable	Embrace it accept it learn from it try again

He's Working It Out
as told by Morris Robinson

Making It Through the Storm

My family has lived here in Gulfport for about fifty years. I moved into my current house in 1972. This had been my mother's home. She had gotten sick, and was not able to do for herself. She did not want to go into a nursing home, so she asked me if I would move back in to look after her. At that time, our four children were still living at home. We were able to move in here and give her a hand. We kept a home with her until she died. Then I made this our home.

We have lived through two major storms since I have been here. The first was hurricane Camille. At that time, I was in the Navy and stationed in Okinawa, Japan. My wife and children were here, and they went into the shelter at the naval base. That storm took the roof off our house. The Lord so blessed us that we were able to get it back on.

The second storm was Katrina. The Friday and Saturday before Katrina hit, we heard on the news that the storm might come in at New Orleans rather than here, between Gulfport and Biloxi, Mississippi. That's what we expected. We did not make any great preparations.

However, when we got up Sunday morning and turned to the weather Channel, the situation was totally different. Instead of the storm going toward New Orleans, it was going to hit between Pascagoula and Gulfport, Mississippi. When I heard this, I had to change my plans.

Originally, I was going to go to church about fifteen miles from here in Bay St. Louis. Another minister was going to come to the church here in Gulfport. But after hearing the report on the storm, I called and told him to stay in Bay St. Louis, and said that I'd stay here in Gulfport. We did what we could to protect our home.

We had no idea that it was going to be that big of a storm and cause that much damage. Around three o'clock on Sunday afternoon we heard that we were asked to leave. I really did not want to go to a shelter, but my wife said that she was going.

I said we should check and see what our daughter and her husband were going to do. My son-in-law said that he was willing to stay with me, but our wives were going to leave and go into a shelter. After a "discussion" on this, we decided that we would *all* go to a shelter. What a blessing it was that we did go with them!

There were some warehouses at the Gulfport Naval Base that were opened up for people who needed shelter. As I had been in the Navy, I felt that I knew their rules a little better, so I felt more comfortable staying at the base. That is the shelter we went to. By nine o'clock on Sunday night, there were about two to three hundred other people in the shelter at the naval base with us.

In the warehouses, the windows were boarded so that we could not see out, but at night, we could hear the wind howling across the building, tents flapping, and the wind blowing the doors. Now, this was a great building with strong doors, but the wind blew them open. We had to move to a different section of the warehouse in order to not get wet.

We stayed in the shelter all day Monday, not really knowing what was happening outside the warehouse doors. During the time in the shelter, people were mostly calm. There was water, coffee, and juice to drink. Movies were shown and popcorn was made. There were games for the children. The chaplain even had a prayer service one night.

We were fed those military sea rations. In fact, it was good. They were better than when I was in the service. When I was in the navy, we had to make a little fire to warm up our sea rations. But the ones they have now, you just pour water into it and it heats itself up. It tasted just like regular food, no different. I really enjoyed it. They gave us that for three meals a day. If you got hungry during the night you could go down and get another one. They made us feel good while we stayed there.

We were kept in the warehouses until Tuesday morning to give a chance for the streets to get cleared and to make sure that there were no live wires on the street. On Tuesday morning, they opened up. We saw that it had hit pretty bad on the naval base. Most of the housing that was built in 1942 was damaged. Those barracks have since been torn down and new ones have been built.

There were several cars that had been damaged, including mine. The cars on the outside of the parking area had more damage than those that were parked on the inside. My car had lots of dents in it and the windows were broken. We could get the windows replaced and the car repainted so we were not too worried about that. We were happy that the car started!

Later that day, after coming off the base, I went down to the beach along Highway 90, which is less than a half mile from where I live. Along the highway, there were big, beautiful, colonial style homes, great restaurants, and other places and businesses. There was nothing left along Highway 90. From Biloxi through Bay St. Louis and Waveland, Katrina took away everything.

Whether your home was destroyed or not, seeing all those homes gone and all the other buildings blown completely away, it felt like it was your home. You began to feel the hurt and the sorrow that those people had out there. You knew that when they came back, they would see nothing.

Well, when I came back and saw my house, at least it was still standing. I did not have any great damage that I could see right off. I just did me a little dance, and thanked God that he had let nothing more happen to our house.

However, as we walked into the house and began to check, we could see that there was some damage. The water had come up under the house through the flooring. It was enough to soak the carpet. The water had also come in through the roof, from one end to the other. The water that came in through the ceiling is how our furniture and other things got wet. Many things were soggy and had to be thrown away right then. We cleaned up as best we could. We thought that everything was all right, but we learned later that it was not.

At first, we had no electricity or gas. The water was also turned off. But, we stayed at our home anyway after we came out of the shelter. We used candles for light. We sat out on the porch with our mosquito protection in place. It was nice. We would sit outside until about midnight or one in the morning. The air was kind of cool then.

It made me think of church, when the people fan themselves. I told them that fanning was really nice. However, I told them not to make any long strokes, just do real short strokes. I found out that that cools you off better than fanning really hard. Just make little waves. It really works.

My daughter's husband was able to get a generator to keep a portable air conditioner running as he is a paralyzed vet. The doctor said that since he was paralyzed, they could get that all fixed up for him. It worked out really well. They wanted us to come over and stay there to keep cool, but I decided to stay at home.

We ate simply. I never used to like canned chili. But, I found out that there is nothing better than canned chili and spaghetti. That's what we had to eat mostly. We had a little arch stove. We could set the can in the pot and warm it up.

Unwelcome Revelation

As things improved and utilities came back, we settled in. Now my children kept saying, "Daddy, why don't you just go ahead and paint those last two rooms, and put new carpet on the floor?" I told them that I did not want to do that. About three weeks later, I heard the same thing. "Why don't you paint those rooms and put in new carpet?" I repeated that I did not want to do that.

In addition, every time our daughter would come in the house she would say, "Mom, I smell mold!" At that time, I didn't think about it, and I didn't smell it, probably because I lived here. But, every time our daughter came she said the same thing.

Then our son came down from Tennessee, and he said, "Dad, are you sure you don't have any mold in here?" I told him that I was not sure.

Then, in March of 2006, I got a cold. My bronchial tubes started giving me problems. It became pneumonia, so I had to go to the hospital. Now we were concerned that we *did* have mold in the house.

We called for an inspector to come to our home to check it out. Unfortunately, he found mold. We could not believe that we had lived in the house for about six months after the storm not knowing we had a mold problem. I was still in the hospital when the mold was discovered, so they checked me out very well. Probably the mold had triggered the pneumonia.

After the inspection, we were told that we had to move out and gut the house completely. We have this blow in type of installation in the ceiling and we had to remove all of it because mold was setting in. We had to get rid of everything. My wife and I reluctantly did as we were told and moved out into a FEMA trailer.

At that time, I did not have any money to fix my house. So, I put in for volunteers to come in and help us. The first group that came was the North Carolina Baptist brothers. A man in this group checked and told me that there was not any mold. I said, "Well, they told me that we have mold and need to gut the entire house." He said that they would gut the house, but insisted that there was not any mold.

They worked from room to room to room, still looking for mold. They did not come in contact with any. Then, in the very last room that they stripped, they found the deep, black mold. That was a blessing!

How was that a blessing? If they had found the mold in the beginning, they would have corrected it, checked for other mold, and finding none, they would have stopped. Then, the rest of the house would have looked the same old way. God placed the mold where He wanted it to be, in the very last room.

I was thankful that I had not listened to that advice from my children to just paint the back rooms, or we would still be in the same situation. The Lord kind of deafened my ears, so I didn't listen. Then, I could follow the leading of God. I did not redo those two back rooms where the mold was found. If I had, I may have covered up the mold, or just have wasted time and money.

The Baptist brothers were very good. They fixed up four rooms for me. This was about a year and a half after the storm. One day they came to tell me that they were about ready to go back to North Carolina. Their volunteer time in this area was at an end. However, I still had four more rooms to go and did not know how I would get it done.

Months of Work, Months of No Work

With the volunteers gone, I went to FEMA and they were able to give me some money. I hired a contractor, and it cost me $14,000 to repair one bedroom and one bathroom. We ran out of money again. So, I asked the Lord how we were going to work it out now. What were we going to do?

Two years passed. Then, I was talking with a minister that I knew, and she said that she might know some people who could help us. She introduced me to the Biloxi Camp at a

Lutheran Church. There I met Marcella, a social worker; Darrell, a job site supervisor; and Tom, a long-term volunteer. They were all very nice people. They came to our rescue and they just blessed us.

When I first came in touch with Camp Biloxi, Marcella told me that they did not have any funds to help me, but they still had volunteers coming in to provide the labor. I was perfectly willing to go along with that. We had some materials that had been given to us right after Katrina to help us fix our house and I had about $4000 left from what FEMA had given me. So, I went with Marcella to Lowe's and made out an account there. That way, the brothers who worked on the house could just go there to get what they needed.

This time the work on our back bedroom and bathroom, which was almost identical to the work I paid $14,000 to have done, only cost about $500. That was because God was in control now! God was in control, and He knew just how to work it out. The work continued.

When we moved out of our home, we lived in a FEMA trailer for the first three years. Then, we moved into a FEMA cottage. It has three bedrooms, but they are very small. It's better than not having any room. However, FEMA had given us a deadline of December 28, 2009. We were to move out by then. That is why we were working hard, trying to meet that deadline. Realistically, there was no way we could move into our home by that time.

We were hoping that following the inspection of the bedroom and bathroom that had been completed in November of 2009, we could move back in. Then, we would just block off the other two rooms, as they wouldn't really affect us, and live in the front part of the house. The work could then continue from the back of the house. However, my wife felt that she really did not want to bring everything here and set up in just one room. So, I just said, "Lord, I don't know what I'm going to do."

I went to speak to someone about our FEMA trailer. I told him that we would not be able to get out by December 28, and I asked him if there was some way he could work with us. He said, "I'll tell you what, I can't tell you how long I can prolong your time, but I'll work with you and I won't put you out. When I feel like I can go no longer, I'll give you at least one week to move out."

You see how God worked there? We were to be out December 28 and it is now January 18, and we are still in the FEMA trailer. The Lord is working the way. And now it is getting close. We have been cleaning up things. So we will be prepared to move back in. It will be a great blessing to get back to our home.

Miracles

Since our time to move back in was getting closer, I went to the cable company. I told them that we were in the storm and that we had cable before that, but we did not have it now. A clerk looked up our account. She said, "That will be $300, and it has to be paid now." I said okay and I left. I knew that I did not have the $300 to give her.

Next, I went over to the phone company to get them to check my phone. After I came out of there, for some reason I had it in my mind to go back to the cable TV place. It really did not make sense to do that, but I felt prompted to go anyway. This time I got a different person. I told her that I was there about getting the cable put back in and to find out when they could do it. The other lady, to whom I had spoken earlier, was sitting, kind of in front of me, and she said, "He came in here this morning." That's all she said.

However, this second woman looked up my account and said, "You know what? I've got some good news. Do you want to hear it?" I assured her that if it was good news, I definitely wanted to hear it. "We owe you, instead of you owing us. Just let me check with my supervisor to make sure."

Then, the supervisor came in and said that she was right. The cable company owed me $178. This money had been due to me for four years! So, I set up an appointment to have it connected again.

When the guy came to my home to install the cable, he asked if I had been told about making a deposit at the time at the time of installation. I said that no one had told me about that. He said that we were supposed to make that payment. I told him that I was not informed about that.

Another gentleman came walking through my front door right behind him, and he said, "Oh no. He doesn't have to do that." I guess the first man saw $178 on the ticket, and he thought I was supposed to give it to them. But, the other guy had the work order and knew that the money was owed *to* us.

Originally, the appointment that I had set up said they were supposed to arrive between noon and five. However, it was about a quarter till five until they got there. After checking the house, the man said, "I'll tell you what, I'm going to have to do some rewiring. If you let me wait until Monday to do it, I won't charge you."

Praise the Lord! "That will be great!" I said. "I'll only be too glad to do that."

He came back on Monday and wired the house for cable. However, he had trouble getting our TV to work. Now this was the TV that we had before the storm, which meant that it had been over four years since we used it. The cable man tried, but he really could not get it to work the way he wanted it to.

While he worked, I was sitting in a chair in the living room trying to remove some paint that had been accidentally splattered on it. The cable man said, "You know what? I have a chair at home that my father had and he only used it for about three months. It's just been sitting there for four months now. Do you want it?"

I said, "Yes, I would be grateful." He went and got the chair. Oh, it is a comfortable, reclining chair. When he returned with the chair, he also brought a TV with him. I asked, "Who's that for?"

He said, "I can't get that one back there to work for you. So, my wife and I decided to go get you one." The old one I had was a twenty-one inch. He brought a forty-inch plasma TV. Something I never had, never owned, and probably would never have bought.

All of this may sound like nothing, but I see God's hand in it. Some people would say to go back to the cable store a second time in the same day would be pointless. It just came into my mind to go back over there. If I had gotten the same person, I might not have been able to get the cable put back in because she most likely would have given me the same answer. Yet, I told the second woman the same thing I had told the first woman. I had not changed my story or made it sound any different. How then did I get a different result?

Now, we had been having very cold weather. It is unusual for us to have days on end where the temperature goes below freezing, but we did. It was the end of December 2009. Some volunteers were asking if it might be possible to have some heat in the house, as it was very cold to work there. I said that I would go down to the gas company to see about having the heat turned on. This was on a Thursday. Money was really scarce for me at this time. I really did not have it. I knew there would be a fee to have the gas turned on, but I thought I would go anyway.

On my way out, I stopped by the mailbox to get in the mail. One piece of mail was from the gas company. I opened it and found that it was a check for $75. I just figured it was some money that they owed me because I had overpaid, or whatever. I stuck it in my pocket and went on to the gas company.

When I arrived, I told the lady that I wanted to put the meter back on in my house and turn the gas on. She typed in my information and said, "That will be $75." I handed her the check. She continued, "I don't know why they would hold a check for three years and just send it now."

In my heart, I began to thank God. I really did not have the $75. I did not have it. But the check was $75. The exact amount I needed. I just handed her the check. God makes ways out of no ways!

One day, the caseworker told me, "Mr. Robinson, we're going to have to talk. Your account is running out of money." I was sitting here by myself thinking, looking out the back window, knowing that the money was again coming to an end. I looked out the window and said, "Lord, *how* am I going to finish it now? *What* are we going to do from here? You know we're running out of money."

Then I heard someone walking toward me, but I didn't pay any attention. Tom came over and put his arm around my shoulder. He said, "Don't worry. The Lord is good. Do you know what? The people that were here two weeks ago sent some money for you to finish the work."

Tears came to my eyes. You see, I was sitting there trying to figure it out myself, not realizing that God had already worked it out. It made my heart feel so wonderful. I told Tom that he was my angel. He said that he wasn't, but I reminded him how God sent an angel messenger to Joseph. He was my angel, because I was down in the gutter and did not know where money would come from and he brought good news. Now, we had some money. He was my angel and it was not just that one time.

God Made a Way

Now, we would be able to finish this back bedroom. This room is for an elderly lady from our church who is in a nursing home. She did not want to go there. I had told her that I would take care of her when she got to the place where she could not take care of herself. I have not been able to do that. But now, when this room gets finished, I can keep my promise.

Originally, this room only had one small window and was very dark. This family who had raised the money for us to finish thought the room needed a second window. Their goal was to raise about $300 to cover the cost of two new windows. Instead, they raised $1300. I said, "Lord, I thank you! You are just working it out!"

Not only did that room get new windows, but the walls on the east and north were taken out and redone. They were made level and strong. That room is new inside and out. The elderly lady who will be staying in this room can say that God put her in a new house. I am grateful to how God worked it out to get my whole house redone.

One day as Tom, my angel, was working on a frustrating problem with my house, he said to me, "Now see what you got me into?"

I said, "Uh-uh, I didn't do that. He did!" I pointed my hand up. "God got you into this. He knew way before Katrina came that you were going to be here today. So, I didn't get you into this. Don't blame me. God got you into this."

Then I thought, "Did I speak the right thing when I said don't blame me, blame God?" That could have been taken another way, like I was boasting. I didn't mean it that way. I did not do anything. It's just that I knew that God had prepared things for me. God had made a way. God prompted Tom to come down from Iowa to Mississippi and work. There was no way Tom could get out of it.

I do not think there has been a sad moment or a moment of disbelief about the house getting rebuilt since I met Tom in the fall of 2009. Some people would say that things are going to happen, however they happen. I know differently.

God has given me blessings and I am grateful. We are grateful and thankful that the Lord sent someone along to help us. I have met many different people who have worked so faithfully with me.

Volunteers

When the volunteers come to work, I just sit around and try to stay out of their way, because I do not want to be a bother. I say, "Look, you know what you need to do. If it needs to be done, you do it. I'm not going to tell you what to do and how to do it. You do it. You are in control of the job. Don't worry about me." I do not get in the way. I want them to feel free to do the work the way they want to do it.

I would say that the volunteers right now are doing a beautiful job. They are working in my home just like if it was their home. They are taking good pains with it. They are correcting a lot of things that some builders before them kind of messed up.

For example, the roof sagged so they built roof beams from the inside to support it to make it better than it was before. The floor was lopsided, but they jacked it up to make it level. They tied and secured the frame for the room. They really put that back bedroom together. If we have a hurricane, I am going to that back bedroom! They have worked hard on that space. In that way, God has really blessed me.

Another improvement is how well our house is insulated. We can set our thermostat at sixty-eight degrees and it feels comfortable. It comes on and off and it's still pleasant in here. We have never been able to have it at that. We usually ran it at seventy-five or seventy-eight degrees. Now, it is so well insulated that it is not like it was. I guess it has never really been insulated. When the air-conditioning was put in, they blew some foam insulation into the ceiling, but the walls had never been insulated.

When I look at the back bedrooms that they are working on now, with all the insulation, I feel like it is padded down.

It may not mean a lot to some, but to me it is solid like a rock, it's so padded down. This is a warm house now. It makes me feel so good to know that it is insulated.

Some volunteers have been ladies. They get in there and they work just like they were men. I guess I have not liberated them yet. I still feel like they shouldn't be in there doing that. But they've done a great job, and I appreciate it.

We also had some young girls come in and lift up heavy things that I could not lift up myself. They could lift those things up and throw them into the dumpster. It would be good to be young again!

Now I have worked with young people at church and I have been around young people, but I've never really met young people that have been so dedicated to God like the young people I have met who have worked on our house. These young people have prayer before they start working. They just talk and enjoy each other. Some of them did not know each other until they came on the job. They just talk like they've known each other for a long time.

I remember when I was cleaning out our personal things back in our bedroom, I told them that whatever they thought needed to be thrown away, throw it away. I told them not to ask me—just throw it away—because I trusted anyone who came to work here. I trust their opinions and their ideas. That is why I love volunteers. And, it has worked wonders!

I trust these people. I have no reason not to trust them. I love people and I love that they speak to God. Have your way, Lord! Have your way! I thank God for all the great people who have come to work here. I am grateful.

Lessons Learned

It has been four years getting our house repaired and it has become very expensive to try to make it look like we want it to look. If I had known how extensive the damage really was on my house, I probably would have just built a whole new home rather than fix this one. That is what my wife wanted me to do. My wife always wanted to live in a new house, but we never did. This whole thing has been hard on her.

Evidently, the Lord did not want me to build a new house, because if He had, we would have gone in that direction. But now, our house is completely new from top to bottom, from ceiling to floor on the inside. Everything in here has been changed.

We have been waiting patiently and the Lord has been working it out. That is what I like most. He has been working out these decisions of anything that gets complicated. While I am back here at the fence getting lost in thought, the Lord comes in, works, and opens up the way.

Actually, I have enjoyed living in that little, small trailer. I didn't worry. I just thanked God for the trailer. I never did complain to God. I was sort of like Job. Even in that time when I was feeling low and just staring into space, wondering where I was going to get the money, I did not complain. I did not say, "Lookee here, Lord, what you got me into. Now you got to get me out of it." I did not look at it that way. I was just looking at *how* I was going to be able to get it, and He let me know when he sent the messenger!

I've got more titles for Tom. He was the angel who gave me the message that he had the funds. I give Tom so many titles. The honest truth is that I kind of hate that the work is coming to an end. I honestly do. I have enjoyed meeting him. I have enjoyed talking with him. I have enjoyed being around him. I really hate that it is coming to the end. I feel that way. That is the sad part, when I think about that. I will not be seeing him.

Volunteers have told me that I am as much a blessing to them as they have been to me. I do not see how that is any way possible. The reason is that they do not know the condition I was in before I met any of them.

I've always been the type of person who is easy-going and easy to get along with, yet I didn't really know what it actually meant to *feel* and to *know* the saying that "God may not come when you want Him, but He will come right on time." To actually know what that means came to me through Tom. To know that God comes to you, even when you do not know when or where or how or what, had a great bearing on me. He comes in and He works it out. He works in such a great way. To me He was saying, "Look. Here."

It's the same thing with that gas check. Why did I get that letter from the gas company on Thursday? Three years later! Why did I get it on Thursday? Why did the volunteers complain that they needed some heat that very day?

Our faith in God has kept us hanging in there. Faith is just so beautiful. I thank God for believing in Him and knowing what He can and will do. We cannot doubt Him. I have found no fault in Him. He has proven Himself to us. I do not see how anyone can say that there is no God. Sometimes He takes you through and you think you've got faith. Then He lets you put it to work to find out if you've really got it. I have had to find that out. Did I really have it?

We live by faith that tomorrow we will be back in our home. Every day will be a tomorrow. We will be back in. That tomorrow seems to be in sight now. We can see it— moving back in. I feel good. I can see me right now walking through this house with everything in its place. I appreciate everything that everyone is doing. May God bless you and keep you!

First Voice Faith Reflections

When these first person stories were collected, there were very few questions asked of the storyteller. Residents were simply directed to share their story, to offer whatever accounting they would like to share. With that opening, the words just spilled forth. Often, hours passed until the tale was told.

Upon transcribing these stories, two commonalities became obvious. One, in every story of those who went through Hurricane Katrina, there was at least one moment of calm, one moment of hope, that allowed the person to persevere. God spoke to their heart in a way that they could hear and receive and be comforted.

For Annette Richard, it was the symbols of her faith that remained untouched, reminding her of God's presence. Hope and peace were given to Nick when he saw three birds flying, reminding him of the Trinity. He clung to the idea of the safety and comfort of home to help him persevere through the long years of recovery, as we long for our eternal home and God's comforting arms.

Mike Kovasevich also maintained hope and courage through reminders of Jesus. The first came at the height of the storm in the image of Christ on the cross created from a cloth trapped in trees. Later, it came from the statue of the Virgin Mary that came to rest on his porch and remains there to this day. Years later, when he encounters those who offered aid in an unexpected place, he is reminded of God's steadfastness.

A multitude of miracles convinced Morris Robinson that God had not deserted him. Unexpected donations of materials from volunteers arrived just when needed. Money necessary to provide heat in the home came in the form of a long overdue rebate check. All things in His perfect timing!

The second commonality was the statement that if not for the volunteers, the people of the Mississippi coast would have nothing. The majority of the volunteers arrived because of, or through faith-based organizations. Other volunteers were sent from colleges and universities. Students came during spring break to tackle hard and dirty work rather than vacation at a resort. Some were individuals who just wanted to help and came on their own. They came from other countries such as Canada and New Zealand.

Gratitude for the thousands of strangers who arrived on the Gulf Coast to help was unending. Thanks were shouted out in restaurants and on the streets. Billboards were posted along the highways offering a written word of thanks. These volunteers were the hands and feet of God to hurting communities.

Second Voice:

Stories of Faith, Endurance, and Transformation

"Seeds of Life"

Seeds that are sowed now
will come to life soon

Echo the sound heard far
and wide

Cloudy days clear nights one
star gleaming
Bright

Blinded by blazing sun, cool
by the evening Winds

Walking, thinking, hoping
for a new south

Walking, thinking, hoping
for a new south

Small town eyes stare and
gaze, whispers hear, whispers
seen

Back to fishing just for fun;
catch them, throw them
back, one by one

Longing to take a swim,
unsure, is it safe

Longing to lay in the grass
and be touched by the sun

Work from sunrise to sunset,
the more you do the more
there is to do

Work from sunrise to sunset,
the more you do the more
there is to do

Night falls again; tired hearts,
bodies and spirits lay down
for a rest

At the end of each day the
question is asked

What keeps us going... the
beauty of a new day

What keeps us going... the
beauty of a new day

The second voices heard are of those who came to help for the long haul. Some of these called the Gulf Coast home. They were compelled to do whatever they could to help their neighbors. Others came from hundreds of miles away to offer extended assistance. The rebuilding that occurs is not only of houses, but of lives.

Tom Fox resides in Davenport, Iowa. After retiring, he was drawn to the coast for months at a time, volunteering his services. In **Unexpected Changes** *he articulates the profound growth in himself and the irony of how God directs one's path.*

A Georgia girl all her life, Jan Freeman shares her own private tragedy that led her to Camp Biloxi as a staff member. **Lost and Found** *illustrates her personal healing in the course of her work, and through God's love expressed to her in those around her.*

Rava Coyle had come to call Biloxi, Mississippi, home. At the time of the storm, she was visiting her mother in Virginia. Her homecoming to Biloxi was surreal. With a heart to help, she begins a path that leads to the growth of Camp Biloxi and beyond. She expresses her journey of following God's will for her in **Jill of All Trades.**

Unexpected Changes
Interview with Tom Fox
Long-term Volunteer

Why did you decide to come to Biloxi to do relief work?

Maybe a little of it started with a former pastor. He and I did not always see eye to eye. I sat down with him one day to talk to him about some issues. I remember that I spoke strongly.

After I went through my speech, he said to me, "You know what you need to do? You need to get involved in something. You need to get involved maybe with Habitat for Humanity." I'm telling him off and he's coming up with this stuff? Right!

A while later, my friend Steve, who has been involved with Habitat for years, called me and asked me to help him with a project. It was through Steve that I got hooked up with coming down to Mississippi. In October of 2006 I took a week's vacation and came down with this group from Habitat for Humanity.

We stayed in East Biloxi. We built a house over in Gautier. One day we had a "rain day," and the husband of this older couple that came down with us said, "Hey, you know, a guy from our church is over at Camp Biloxi. I want to go over to see him."

I did not know who the guy was, but I said that I would go along with him. We drove over to Camp Biloxi and met some people there. For some reason or other, at that point, I thought to myself that I needed to come back here. I was thinking about the vacations that we did with the boys and thought it would be so cool if we all came down here and did this.

A few months later my wife, Judy, said, "Why don't we go to Camp Biloxi during spring break?" So, we came down and spent a week here in March of 2007.

I came here and met these people and thought, "Yes, this is where I want to come!"

I retired, December 31, 2007. I was here, January 19, 2008 until Easter. Judy joined me on her spring break that year. Occasionally, I would fly home for a bit. I came back down off and on over the next year. March of 2009 my wife came back down with a group from our church and joined me. She came back at Easter and she also joined me here in July of 2009, spending the month.

Spending the month of July in Biloxi was a good idea, but not a good idea. It was a good time, but it was rather warm. Then I went home for a month or two, came back in October, and stayed for another few months.

In thinking about how I came to be here, it is kind of ironic. I was just railing at that former pastor, but he said something to me that got me started on the path that I am on now. I don't like to give him any credit, but it's true. Although what sealed it was when my friend Steve simply asked me to help him.

Why do you keep coming back to do recovery work?

I have been to other camps, but this is where I keep returning. Sometimes I think that I won't come back, but I do.

I always feel guilty leaving my wife. But, she says that she is very proud of me. I remember the first year that I was here long term. She said how great it was to hear me tell her over the phone that I had a good day. She said that she had not heard that from me in a long time.

I had a neighbor get pretty angry with me because I leave her. I told him to talk to my wife about it because she supported me. I think Judy and I talk to each other more now on the phone then we talked to each other when I was home.

Why do I come back? Some of it is the changes in the homeowners from when we first start working on their home until we are done. At the beginning, many people are depressed. They rarely smile. That is different by the time we finish with the house.

Pastor Robinson said to me the other day that he has not had a bad day since I started working on his home. You know, the way he talks about me is really kind of embarrassing. He sees me as his "angel" who looks out for him and who makes sure things get done. I guess you could say he sees the best of me. He sees a better person than what I think I am.

Also, to see the changing dynamics of the other volunteers that we work with is neat. When the volunteers first start, they are usually more quiet, and naturally so. But, at the end of their time we're all just smiling and having a good time. I enjoy seeing the change in them.

Another reason I guess I come back, honestly, is because I can do something I like and I don't have to pay for the material. Maybe, that is some of it. I get a good feeling doing this work. For the most part, I enjoy the people that I work with. The people here, both the organization and the homeowners, are very respectful of me and I feel like they trust me. I cannot give you a real magical reason why I do this. It has made me feel good. I have definitely changed.

How has working here changed you?

It has changed my marriage, because I'm not as angry and judgmental. I don't get as angry as I used to. I have a horrible, horrible temper, but I do not get near as angry now. I have gotten to the point where I can kind of say "So what?"

I am not as judgmental. I have found people who will come down here with all good intentions, being judgmental. I guess I saw myself in those people. I don't understand it. I am still judgmental to a degree but not to the people here.

I have had so many people ask, "Why are we working on this person's house? They don't need help." Tell me that you lose everything and then tell me that you do not need help!

I do not have to be as tough as I used to be. Working as a probation officer, you have no other choice. I had to be tough. There was no such thing as trust. I told my wife a long time ago that when you start working in the garbage, you start smelling like garbage.

Because of the people I associated with in my work, I can think with a criminal mind. I have had to look at things differently. I had to look at how someone might try to rip you off. I have seen a little of that here. Sometimes, there are

144

people who are milking the system, but you are asked to do a job, and you do it.

In the past, I did not always see who I was. For example, we became really close to our sons' football coach and his wife and other people involved with the team. We got to talking one time and the wife of our son's football coach told me that her first impression of me was that I was hard and intimidating. My wife agreed. She claimed that anyone you would ask about me would say that I was intimidating. I never saw that.

Working here has taught me patience, because not everything has to be done "right now." You do not have to just hurry up and get things done. You can take your time to get it done. It has given me more confidence in doing things that I would have never done before, or even thought of doing before.

For example, our son was asking me about coming down to Florida to his home to change the garage service door for him. That is a big thing for him, but it's no big deal for me. Cut it out. Put it in. Two or three years ago, that would have been a big deal for me, too, just because I was not used to doing that sort of thing. I have learned some things.

I am not as pessimistic. I was born a pessimist and I will die a pessimist. I still think the glass is half-empty rather than half full. I have not given that up. But, when it comes to the Gulf Coast and when it comes to things that happen here, it's different. I have said before that relief organizations are hurting for both money and volunteers. Yet the people that we do get are really good. They see the need, and the money appears.

When you see things like volunteers going in and working on a home and finding out that money is needed to complete the next step of the project and then they donate that money, you know God is at work. At one home, people kept going there and working, money for materials ran out, and then all of a sudden there was money to continue.

At another home, the room we were working on had one small window. A volunteer said, "Wouldn't it be nice if they had two windows? How much would it cost?" When they found out it would cost about $200 or $300, they returned home to raise the money and got more than enough. It makes me think of the five loaves and two fish. Stuff like that has given me more belief in people.

When I see college groups that keep returning, and high school groups that keep coming back, I'm impressed. For some of those kids it was their third time down here. They are not just coming down to play. They are hard workers. I was touched when a young group leader gave me his favorite hat. It was a hat that his father had given him. It is those kinds of things that make my time here worth it. That is payment!

I care more. Everything is relative. What is horrible to me may not be to someone else. However, what happened here—I don't care who you are—was horrible. What happened in Haiti is horrible. I am finding it kind of interesting that I'm thinking of going to Haiti. I would never have thought of that before. My attitude would just be, "Who cares?"

I am not a particularly religious person. That is the other thing that has changed. For me to sit down and say, "Let's say a prayer." Where the heck did that come from? I'm generally not that kind of person. Obviously, there is something or somebody pulling the strings.

I used to be so ticked off at the church. I thought of church people in general as being really hypocritical. So I don't know if it's because I came here or what, but that's changed. In August, we went to our church council and asked for $2000 to help a family purchase drywall and insulation. I said that if we could do that I would go there and hang it. We were told that we could do a special collection. We got $2500 in two weeks.

Is this how you imagined spending your retirement?

I don't know. When my parents retired, they went to South Texas. My dad retired before mom did. (That is the way it is with me. I retired before my wife.) He would spend the winters down there. He told my mom that she could come with him or she could stay home. My sister lived there too and he would just hang out or do work on her place. I saw my retirement as doing some traveling. I did not really have an exact plan.

I just wanted to be done with my years of probation work. I had enough of that environment. I had thought about maybe going to work. Sometimes, what I do here in Biloxi seems like work when we have big groups of people, especially if they are people who are lacking skills and you are trying to get something done. You try to show them how to do things and then they are asking you three or four things at once. I'm not a really good multi-tasker. By the end of the day, I'm worn out.

The only thing I said, when I retired, was that I did not want to work with people. Obviously, that has not been the case. I said I would raise hogs and then if they ticked me off I would kill them. At least they would be worth something! That was my attitude.

Now, continuing to do this kind of work is something that my wife and I would both like to do after she retires in another three years. Just watching other couples work together reminds me of how it will be when Judy and I can do this together. We will be arguing with each other about a job. It's like one wife commented the other day when working with her husband, "Apparently, I'm hard to work with!" This couple had been married for over forty years, and found a way to work through their different opinions. That will be Judy and I.

Actually, I feel a little bit envious of couples who can do this right now. When Judy retires, I hope that we will be in good enough health to do this work. As there is a time for everything, if this camp closes, I am willing to go anywhere help is needed. I would miss Camp Biloxi. This organization has really got its act together.

I like what a fellow worker here said, "Take away south Mississippi and you can go anywhere in the United States and do mission work. You don't have to go to a foreign country." The work, the people, and the homeowners have brought about these changes in me.

Lost and Found

Interview with Jan Freeman
Assistant Camp Director, Camp Biloxi

How did a Georgia girl come to work at Camp Biloxi in Mississippi?

I don't know. One day I came to myself and I thought, "Where am I? How did I get here?" I had been in shock. People told me that I went through the motions of everyday life and seemed to be fine, but nothing really sank in. I had experienced a horrible tragedy and it had nothing to do with the storm.

Are you comfortable sharing what happened?

Well, for all my life, it was just my daddy, my brother and me. My mother left us when I was three and my brother was five months old. I loved my daddy dearly. As adults, the three of us continued to live together.

Although I had a boyfriend and had been engaged to be married for eight years, I felt the need to take care of my daddy. I had been the one to do everything at home for both my father and my brother. It was hard to stop doing that. My daddy eventually retired as sheriff, but took a job as court bailiff in order to have something to do. Then, he got cancer.

I wanted him to walk me down the aisle, so I set a wedding date. Unfortunately, he died in August of 2007 before the wedding date arrived.

The day of his viewing, I went to the funeral home first to make sure everything was arranged. My brother and my fiancé were going to join me around four-thirty. The time came and went. People arrived and went. Still, they did not show up. I was getting mad. Where could they be? Why would they let me alone like this? I tried calling them but no answer.

Around eight, a friend of my daddy's called me aside. He said that he had something to tell me. It seems that there had been a head on collision between a tractor-trailer truck and my brother's truck. Both my brother and my fiancé had been killed. In an instant, I had lost my entire family. I had no one else. I was totally alone in this world.

I only know what happened and how I ended up here by what I was told by other people.

So, how did you end up here?

My daddy had a good friend who moved to Ocean Springs, Mississippi, after the two of them retired. The friend and his wife moved there in order to look after her parents who lived there. My daddy would visit them in Ocean Springs or Mr. Graham would come here to go hunting and fishing with my daddy.

They had come back to Georgia for my daddy's funeral. When the tragedy happened, they took me in. They decided that it would not be a good idea for me to be by myself, so they brought me back with them to Mississippi to stay for a month or two.

Miss Sarah, who took me in, is friends with Miss Phyllis at Good Shepherd Lutheran Church. That's how she heard that Camp Biloxi needed a cook.

Then you were looking for a job?

No. I did not know that I wanted a job, but it found me! The Grahams found me a little apartment in Biloxi. It was a little over a mile from the camp. I had no car. I walked to the camp at three in the morning along the dark streets in order to start cooking breakfast for the volunteers.

I lived there for about a month when Tom B. stopped in to drop off something for me. He returned to camp to explain to the camp director where I lived and the distance I had to walk in the middle of the night. The very next week, Bob R. had an RV on camp for me to live in.

I cooked for a few months and then I worked as an assistant camp director. That involved greeting the volunteers, giving them an orientation to the camp and to the area, cleaning the facilities, and in general, making sure the volunteers had a good experience in camp. I have always been able to talk with people. That's the Georgia girl in me. I guess I did all right with the volunteers, but I don't remember much.

How did working here help you?

As I said, at first I did not really remember very much. However, being here helped me to feel safe. I would often sleep during the daytime because I knew that other people were awake and I knew they would keep an eye on me. At night, I would stay awake because I knew that everyone else was asleep. That's often when I would clean the bathrooms and showers.

I did not leave the grounds of the camp for several months. I had bad days where I would just cry and feel depressed. When that happened, Matt, my boss, would just tell me to go to my RV for a spell. I could just let him know that I was having a bad day, and he would take care of everything.

The boys who worked here were real good to me. I knew that they had my back and would look out for me. They did not force me to do anything if I was having a bad day.

After time in my RV, I would feel better and could do my job again. Other than that, I never took any time off. I did some work around the camp almost every day of the week. Vacation days piled up.

I just love my volunteers! I called them "my volunteers" because it was my job to look out for them and I did everything in my power to do just that. I got to meet and know many really nice people. They made me feel good, especially when we would joke and carry on. The ones that came back several times began to feel like family to me.

Little by little, I began to heal. A homeowner whom we had helped got his sister to donate her old Volvo to me. With a car, I ventured off the camp grounds just down the road to the Walmart. I started to sleep more at night. But, I still couldn't get myself to go home to Georgia. Everything there remained as it was.

I could not have had better people around me. I knew that they would look out for me and help me. I am not so afraid anymore.

What are your plans for the future?

I know that I have to deal with my father's things back in Georgia. I did manage to go there for a few weeks in March of 2010. I visited the graves and tidied them, but it was still too hard and I left. Georgia just did not feel like home any more.

I am not sure what the future holds for me. I know Camp Biloxi will not be here forever. I don't know where I'll go. I have had invitations from people to come and work and live with them from California to Pennsylvania. I have met good people and have made great friends, so I do not feel totally alone. The horrible tragedy that happened here on the Gulf Coast helped me to find myself again. I was lost for a while, but now I am finding my way.

Jill-of-all Trades

Interview with Rava Coyle
Volunteer Coordinator, Camp Biloxi

Just to give us some background—to place the setting— where were you when Katrina hit the Gulf Coast?

I was in my hometown in Virginia. My mom had had open-heart surgery, and I was there with her. Our daughter was living in Massachusetts at the time, but my husband and son were in Biloxi. I had tried to come back on Sunday, the day before the storm was to hit, but all the flights were canceled and we could not come back. So, after the storm, my husband and son left Mississippi and drove to Virginia, before I returned.

My husband was actually hospitalized in Virginia. Right after the storm, he took a shower at home in Biloxi, not realizing the water was contaminated. He still had an open incision from a surgery earlier in the year and it became infected. So, he was in the hospital on one floor and my mother was on another floor. He was in the hospital for about three days receiving IV antibiotics.

After he got out of the hospital, my husband and son gathered everything they could and headed back to Biloxi. I flew back within two weeks of the storm.

When flying over the coast, you saw a lot of blue tarps. There was a lot of debris with a lot, a lot, a lot of cleaning up to do. You did not see many things that you should have. Everything was gone. Even today, it is hard for me to drive along the coast. It's just gone. Things that are supposed to be there are gone.

The day I returned, my husband and son picked me up. We dropped my suitcases at home and went to our church. There was already a distribution center in the fellowship hall. We started helping right away. We dug right in. We just walked into it.

The first people who came to help arrived the day after the storm. They had come from Florida. They were staying in the church for several days and I helped to cook for them. The year before, Florida had had three hurricanes and they *knew* what we needed. These volunteers came right away, with exactly what we needed. That was a true blessing.

How did you come to do the job of volunteer coordinator for Camp Biloxi?

To begin with, I filled all sorts of positions. I started out in the distribution center. Early on, we would go home at night and review the work request forms that people had filled out. We would call them to see if anyone else was helping them or if they still needed help. I remember that first Thanksgiving, feeling so sad after talking to one woman on the phone. She said, "I wish you had called me before, maybe y'all could have helped. But they knocked my house down."

I have gone out with construction guys when they've done estimates and took pictures. I have cooked in the kitchen. I have cleaned in the bathrooms. I have unloaded the trucks. I have done spiritual and emotional care. I have worked with the volunteers. In April after the storm, we opened the Greenhouse as our main office. I worked as the office manager.

I volunteered for about seven months until it became a paid position for me. Now, I am a paid staff member. When I am asked for a job description, I put down "Jill-of-all trades." Whatever needs doing is what I do.

So, this has been an evolving process.

It still is, because no one has ever really dealt with devastation of this magnitude before in this country, at least in the times that anyone who is alive can remember. It is a learning process and it evolves daily. You never know what tomorrow is going to bring. You just get up and roll with it.

When you come back and you see this devastation, and you are blessed to still have your family, and your home, and your church, and your church family—you cannot stand around with your hands in your pockets. You just step up. That's the way I have always felt. We were put here to help each other. You never know what that really means, but this is how it has turned out for my husband and me. We are blessed to be able to do this every day.

At times it is overwhelming. But then you go talk to the volunteers or the homeowners and they say something that just brightens your day. You are like, "You know, we're doing this for all the right reasons. God is good and He's gotten us this far." We just keep going.

My husband and I both feel called to do this work. We feel very blessed that we are even able to do this. So many people need help. Even if you are not able to fix a person's home, knowing that someone cares makes all the difference in a person's life. I can do that part. John and I running this camp can help the volunteers go out and do that as well. That is what we are working for. Just to share God's love with people.

What have you observed or learned in your time about the volunteers, as the volunteer coordinator for this recovery ministry?

Well, I have observed that there are two types of volunteers. There are those who come with a servant's heart, and those who come with a preset way of how it has to be. I think, usually, about 95% of the time, there is one kind of volunteer that leaves here. That kind is a volunteer with a servant's heart.

Once volunteers get here and understand the process and what is going on, they realize that we do the best we can. Once they learn that we are governed by the state of Mississippi and the city of Biloxi and Gulfport and the county and that there are rules and regulations that we have to follow and abide by, they understand.

We want to put people's homes back like we would put our momma's home back. We do not want to do it halfway or not up to standard. We do not want to cause any more problems.

The volunteers of all ages are just very inspirational to me. That first spring break we had over five hundred kids from colleges in a month. All you ever see on TV about spring break is Panama City, and wild and crazy stuff going on. But these kids cared enough to come here and to help us.

I think coming here to help is a life-changing event. It was for everyone on the coast. And, I think it is for everyone who comes to help us. I really do. As bad as Katrina was, there really has been so much good. We are grateful to have been a part of that good in any little way.

You mentioned that you have been involved with spiritual and emotional care. What has that looked like?

It's called the Extra Mile Ministry.[5] Extra Mile was started after 9/11 by Pastor Ralph Buchhorn from San Diego, California. He was actually in Biloxi before I got back here from Virginia. He flew into Pensacola, Florida, and came to Biloxi from there. He was here the first week after Katrina, and he faithfully returned over the next four years.

He was truly such a blessing to us. He had worked at the Pentagon after 9/11. He had a pastoral background and a police background, so he really knows how to deal with people in critical, stressful settings. He taught us a lot about spiritual and emotional care. He came with his dog, Georgie, on several occasions.

The ministry uses golden retrievers as compassion dogs. When you go out with a dog to a home or to a restaurant, or even walking around in the camp, people see the dog, want to know about the dog, and want to pet the dog. People are attracted to golden retrievers. We call it our "calling card." Once people start talking to the dog, they start talking to you. They just open up. Then, you can ask the person how they are doing and what they need. Often, that person will just pour their heart out to you.

There was a tornado in Alabama about a year and a half after Katrina. At the time, Pastor Ralph was here in Camp

Biloxi. Four of us joined him and went to Alabama with two dogs. Just watching the people was amazing.

Some of it is very sad, but at the same time, you keep in your mind that you are helping people. We also have time when we debrief to help us deal with the sadness. For example, when we were in Alabama, there was a large high school that had been hit. Cars were being removed from the school parking lot. The cars that were taken away that day were so damaged that they had to put them on trucks because their wheels would not roll. They had them up on trucks taking them away.

On the other side of the street from the school was a big Baptist Church. They invited us in. They were serving lunch for all the volunteers. As we looked into the gymnasium of the church, we saw all these brown paper grocery bags. Pastor Ralph asked what was in the paper bags. The contents of each of the students' lockers had been removed and placed into a paper bag.

The kids would come in to find their bag and they were crying. That was a very hard experience. But, the kids would come in and pet the dogs and sit down and talk with us. This was totally out of the box, but it worked.

This experience convinced me that I needed to get a dog. I had to get a dog! I talked to my husband and Pastor Ralph about it. I talked about it with other team members. So, the search started for my dog. That was about a seven-month process.

In that time, the shootings at Virginia Tech occurred. We went there about three weeks after it happened, which was near the end of the school year. They asked us if we could come back when school started again, because it would be very hard for students to return to campus.

So, we went back. We worked with a group from New York who had worked at the Twin Towers after 9/11. They had five golden retrievers who they called the smile retrievers. They let me use one of their dogs while we were there, named Macy.

As my own kids had been in band and I was a band mom for eight years, I gravitated to the band room on campus. Although it was sometimes difficult for the students to talk with their family at home about the shootings, they easily talked to us with the dogs.

When we returned again around the year anniversary, I had a girl tell me that if it wasn't for us coming with the dogs, she would not have been able to graduate. That really affected me.

The Extra Mile Ministry is unusual and people do not think about it, but once you are around the dogs you see how it works. I was eventually able to go to California and get my own dog, Honey. Honey and I worked at the shootings at NIU. She also works at the nursing home, she comes to church, and she works at the preschool.

It's touch therapy. It is that "calling card" when people are just ready to share what is going on. A lot of times that's just what people need, someone to listen. Then they will say, "Will you pray with me?" Then we say that yes, we will pray with them.

It is a very wonderful outreach, the Extra Mile, and we are exactly what it says. We go that extra mile. It is that little bit of extra that no one quite thought of. It's really amazing to watch. This is a calling for me too. I am very blessed. I know that. God is good and I give Him all the glory. It is all about Him.

What are some concerns you have for the future?

The preschool where I work is at a very good point, thank the Lord. We have come back. We have room for thirty preschoolers and this year we have twenty-six. We have a wonderful staff. We have a new pastor.

However, the children I am worried about are those who were five, six, seven and eight who survived Katrina but did not understand Katrina. There are some really heart wrenching stories.

There was one little boy who wanted to keep all of his toys in the car. His mother told him that since they have a place to stay now they could keep them in the house with the family. He repeated that he wanted to keep them in the car. When she asked him why he wanted to keep everything in the car, he said that in case the storm came in the middle of the night, he could take everything with him.

I don't know long-term how we're going to handle this, how any of us really long-term will handle it. I think a lot of people are suffering from post-traumatic stress syndrome. A lot of people have not sought help. There are many people who still have not touched their home four years after the storm. You have to deal with it. You really have to deal with it at some level, at some time. Those are my concerns for the children and adults who are the survivors of Katrina.

When another hurricane comes into the Gulf, you can see it on their faces. What are we going to do? Where are we going to go? Out of Katrina, I do believe a lot of good has come. Hopefully, we have learned. Hopefully, we will evacuate. We know how to evacuate. We know we can take our pets. There are some people who died because they thought they couldn't take their pets with them and so they stayed.

So, hopefully we have learned. When someone needs help, we will go help them, whether they are in Mississippi or Virginia or Pennsylvania or California or Iowa. We just need to be thinking more about helping our neighbors.

My husband and I have learned so much that we would like to be able to share that with others. Now, I am not going to walk in anywhere and say, "You must do this, this, and this." But, you can share what you've seen work.

That was just like what Tim Brown from Lutheran Disaster Response did with us. He came to help us set up a volunteer camp. He shared things that have worked before in other places. Working together, using his experience with what we knew we had here, he suggested things to try.

If we can help people in that way, we are more than willing to share what we have learned. When you learn things like this, you need to help people with it. Who knows where that will take us!

Second Voice Faith Reflections

All those who thought they were coming to help were blessed in return. Whether the long-term volunteers and staff members made a conscious choice to come to Biloxi, Mississippi, or they ended in this place by seeming happenstance, all saw the hand of God at work and faithfully followed His direction.

Tom Fox changed into the man God intended him to be. His transformation began ironically. It started with direction from a man with whom he had expressed differences. Thus began a path that would change him. The anger and bitterness he sometimes felt was washed away with the shared tears of loss. His heart melted at the brokenness he witnessed and was renewed with compassion. He was considered a blessing and an angel to those whose lives he touched. He acted as the hands and feet of Christ.

During a time of aloneness and despair, Jan Freeman found a home at Camp Biloxi. It was here that God used the other staff members and the multitude of volunteers to bring her comfort, heal her hurting heart, and give her a place to call home. The volunteers became the family for which she longed. Fellow workers provided a cocoon of protection for her that was like the arms of God wrapped around her. God had not forgotten her. He was faithful.

Rava Coyle simply knew she had to help. She was not always sure what that might look like, but she knew she had to do something. She had faith that God would guide her steps and put her in the right place at the right time. She was His willing servant and she trusted Him to lead.

Third Voice:

Stories of Faith, Service And Commitment

"Clean Up"

Assess the damage, adjuster arrive

Roofs replaced sturdier than before

Sheet rock covering opening

Ceilings renewed

Windows replaced

Windows replaced

Siding put up in many different colors

Chimneys, fireplaces blazing again

Painting completed room by room

Doors being rehung

Beautiful flooring

Beautiful flooring

New wooden cabinets

Personal property regained

Trees planted, flowers coming to life

Smiling, smiling as life continues to gel

Workers taking pride in their work

Workers taking pride in their work

Mail arriving slowly

Encouraging words received

Conversation in all different languages fills the air

Breaks taken, rest while reflecting the

Celebrations of life

Celebrations of life

Good intentions and great expectations may be the same and work together for a smooth result. However, sometimes they are at odds. **Listening and Responding** *describes the good results of conflict when God's hand is involved and when a faithful follower listens.*

The volunteers who poured into the coast had willing hearts, but sometimes lacked skills. That made no difference. All who came had work to do. Each played his own part. Denny in **Rebuilding and Building** *saw that first hand.*

We reach a place in life when we think we have things figured out. Life experiences have shaped us to a point where we believe we have the necessary wisdom to know what choices are best. Then, God surprises us with new twists and unexpected turns. Any age is ripe for new experiences and growth as **Learning and Relearning** *demonstrates.*

Giving and Receiving *is a summation of the collective experience of those who volunteered their time and talents on the Gulf Coast. Although each person's experience was unique, there were common threads that bound the volunteers together. Such a powerful encounter impresses one's heart forever.*

A variety of reasons compelled people from across the nation to travel to the Gulf Coast to help with the work of rebuilding homes, as expressed in **Coming and Going (and Coming and Going).** *They originated from the Northeast, the Midwest, the South, the West and everywhere in between. From teenagers to octogenarians, they appeared at the recovery camps. They got there by airplane, bus, car, van and train. They arrived with faith that they could do something. They came with one purpose—a heart to help.*

Listening and Responding

"My computer's not wireless and there's no internet plug. How can I keep up the blog for the folks at home?" This was Jane's first trip to the Gulf Coast to help with rebuilding efforts. She had worked hard to organize this trip for a group from her church. Everything was in place and ready to go. She was excited!

"You're welcome to come use our computer. We have an air card to receive internet, so you can just bring up the site you want and post your blog. Stop by our RV anytime," Sue called from the other side of the dining tables.

"Thanks! I'll be over right after dinner." Jane knew how to work efficiently. She was not opposed to working hard and expected others to have her same attitude. The blog she uploaded that evening gave a humorous and inspiring account of the daylong drive to the camp and their arrival.

The next day, the first day of the volunteer workweek, Jane informed Sue that she would no longer need to use her air card as an internet cable had been found for her. Sue assured Jane that if she happened to need the use of her computer again, she should just stop by.

Jane was eager to get to the job site and dig in. She had visions of making a major impact on the progress in the Gulf Coast, at least in any home on which *she* worked.

Her day soon fell apart. She was frustrated with the way the work was organized and the pace at which work proceeded. She could see a much clearer way to operate that would be much more productive.

At the end of the day, she marched up to the building that housed the operations center for the organization and strongly shared her frustration and opinion. This was not what she expected at all! She knew what should be done and how to do it.

Later, as she shifted her thinking to what to write on the blog, she discovered that the internet cable she had been promised was "temporarily misplaced." One more irritation! She remembered that Sue had offered the use of her computer again, so Jane headed off to Sue's RV.

When Sue opened the RV door to welcome Jane inside, Jane realized that there was a group of people in the RV with Sue. "Oh! You're busy. Never mind. I can come back later," Jane quickly exclaimed.

"That's fine! Come on in! You are welcome to sit at the table with the computer while we have our devotions. That's not a problem," Sue reassured her. Wanting to be able to check off at least *one* thing from her list, Jane thanked Sue and stepped in.

While Jane worked on her blog, she could not help but overhear the conversation in the RV. What was that she just heard? Meeting God in the ruins? Coming with a servant's heart? We come here to do whatever needs to be done, not what we *think* needs to be done? Oh my!

Jane opened her ears of faith and was immediately convicted. She realized that she had been operating from the mindset of her own desire to excel and accomplish, rather than to yield to another's need.

Jane stopped what she was doing and just sat and stared, wide-eyed. God was speaking right to her heart; He knew her compassion and strong desire to help. God was providing a little fine-tuning to make the best of her efforts. It was her choice to respond or not.

As the group rose to pray, Sue reached out a hand to Jane and invited her to join them in prayer. Smiling, Jane stood to join the circle. As she clasped hands with the group, she confessed, "This is a God thing! I needed to hear this devotion."

The next day went much smoother. Jane was less frustrated. Good work was accomplished. The difference was that those who labored together felt encouraged and blessed to strive side by side.

Rebuilding and Building

Denny remembers his first experience in Biloxi, Mississippi, stationed there in the Air Force in 1966. During his time at Keesler Air Force base, he came to know the kindness of the people in the area and came to appreciate the beauty of the landscape.

After Hurricane Katrina, when he heard his pastor suggest that a group of congregational volunteers go to the Gulf Coast to help with the rebuilding efforts, Denny agreed quickly, remembering with fondness his Gulf Coast experiences of years before. "I thought it was a one-time thing," Denny said, "and initially I agreed to do it because I had a friend down there, and I wanted to do what I could to help."

Before that first trip, Denny did not envision the seven (and counting) subsequent trips that he would make as a volunteer to the Gulf Coast. Why has he returned? In his own words, and simply put, "the job's not finished." He continues, "As long as we can, I'm going to try to get people to go down. My commitment is to get Biloxi straightened out; personally, I'm pushing for that."

While Denny celebrates and even jokes about new skills learned during these experiences ("I'm getting good at 'jacking up' a house"), he also realizes that something else new is happening in the lives of the dozens of volunteers who have shared in these trips with him. In their contributions to the rebuilding effort, they are experiencing their own personal "building up." Denny recalls those who initially say, "I don't know what I can do," to which he responds, "Don't worry, there is something you can do, and be proficient about it."

"I saw people who were not afraid once they had some direction..." and thus the building begins. Denny uses his management skills to develop teams, placing skilled and less skilled workers together, and yielding remarkable results. Different skill sets, different personalities, are teamed with one another for one purpose—to help the people in the Gulf Coast. Denny reports that among these groups there has been little or no complaining, unless they do not have something to do. Given the magnitude of the task, however, there has always been something that has needed to be done. And, Denny reports, he has not heard one person say that they would not return to help again.

Like many volunteers who have returned on multiple occasions, Denny has discovered for himself and facilitated for many others the building of confidence, character, and faith that has occurred time and time again in the rebuilding efforts. Volunteers take from the experience the satisfaction of being part of a most worthwhile endeavor. They take home valuable skills learned and precious memories made. And, like Denny, they feel personally involved and share a stake in the successful rebuilding of homes and lives in the Gulf Coast.

Learning and Relearning

Ken knew how to handle a high energy youth group. That was his job. But this group of geriatrics? This was a completely different situation. They talked incessantly and moved at their own pace—slow! Well, that was not too different from teenagers, but these were adults.

Ken would stand by the bus door at the end of the workday with brows furrowed and impatient sighs escaping his lips, motioning with his hands and calling for his passengers to "come on." They took forever-saying goodbye each day to newly made friends. There was always some story that someone needed to tell or some question to be answered. Then, while some were finally climbing on board, Ken would walk to the back of the van to load materials, and some others would get back off. It was like trying to herd cats!

Other volunteers in camp thought that this whole group of workers between the ages of fifty-seven and eighty-two had such lovely, positive spirits. They were an inspiration to anyone who worked with them. They knew how to enjoy the moment at hand. They were not going to be rushed, but deeply drank in every experience.

At age seventy-five, Myrtle strongly believed, "I have two hands and two feet. So, I gotta help people!" Doris, who was sixty-eight, wanted to learn to use every power tool on which she could get her hands. Ellie said that she did not really need to use her walker. She stated that she just brought it along in case she wanted a seat. Sally was full of questions. She had an appetite to learn that extended from the task at hand to local geography to nature's wonders. Earl, as the eldest member of the group, enjoyed the extra bonus of spending time with his son who accompanied him on the trip.

Ken experienced other struggles. He felt that the group was given demeaning tasks to do. They mostly sanded things like the old porch railings that were being reused, or the steps of the stairs to which a previous volunteer had over-zealously applied wood caulk. He felt that little was accomplished in these jobs.

For example, Sally had spent two and a half days sanding the stairs. Ken was vocal about the menial task she was doing. However, Sally delightfully grinned from ear to ear when complimented on the painstaking job she had accomplished. A site supervisor shared with Ken that someone needed to do that job. If it was not Sally, he would be doing it himself. He explained that *every* job is important and needs to be done. Ken was somewhat appeased.

Little by little, Ken's attitude began to change. As he observed his group dig in to whatever assignment they were given, his expression became thoughtful. His face relaxed. He smiled more often. He eventually gave up trying to rush them along. Instead, he waited patiently.

When the workweek ended, there was much rejoicing in the time spent together. Earl, who was eighty-two, thanked the other volunteers for being patient with him. Everyone was hugging, exchanging email addresses and saying goodbye.

Everyone that is, except for Ken. He hung back, feeling a little awkward at the display of emotion. He wavered between joining in and fleeing.

A fellow volunteer approached him and offered a hug. With a slight frown and self-conscious uncertainty, Ken stiffly reciprocated. The volunteer thoughtfully commented, "This week really stretched you, didn't it?"

With a slight hesitation, Ken acknowledged that indeed it had. Deep in thought, his facial expression changed. There was a new softness to his face. With a sigh of resignation, a look of acceptance with an inner struggle replaced his frown. It was as if he had reconciled old perceptions with a new outlook. It was an outlook that promised new growth.

Giving and Receiving

New groups of volunteers arrived each Sunday at Camp Biloxi. Some groups were large, comprised of twenty plus people. Others had only two members. There were also individuals who came on their own, determined to do whatever was necessary.

As they pulled into camp by car or truck or van or bus, each group was greeted by a camp staff member and directed to their sleeping quarters. At first, the sleeping quarters were huge tents that contained seventy sets of bunk beds. Everyone found a spot that suited. Those who preferred more solitude might erect some blanket or folding wall to separate the space, but no one complained. After time, the tents were replaced with railroad cars that had been converted into sleeping compartments with bunks for two to eight people, which allowed for more privacy.

As vehicles were emptied and sleeping bags unrolled, laughter filled the air as volunteers joked with one another. Many of them had just spent twelve to twenty hours together traveling to get to the Gulf Coast. The camp hummed with activity as each new group settled in.

Questions were called out about facilities and procedures and where to go and what to do. Answers were received at the evening's orientation held in the dining tent where all the volunteers from Pennsylvania or Michigan or Wisconsin or Illinois or California or Maine or Iowa or from almost every state in the Union gathered together. A large United States map stuck with bead-headed pins indicated all the towns and cities across the United States from where volunteers hailed.

A hush fell over the crowd of two hundred as instructions for how to live in this place together for the next week were explained. Gazing over the crowd, there were college students on break who chose to come to Biloxi to work rather than relax or party on a tropical beach. Their strong young backs and high energy were especially needed for some of the dirtier jobs of clearing and cleaning.

Middle-aged volunteers gave of themselves by leaving children and spouses in the care and support of friends and family at home. It had been a chore just to organize everything and everyone at home to make the trip possible. However, they were willing to make the personal sacrifice to be here.

Retired folks showed up and often stayed longer than a week. They gave a stability and wisdom to the work force. Although they may have needed a little more time to complete a task or a few more breaks during the workday, they became a moderating influence when younger folks became impatient or over-zealous.

There were the groups with skilled laborers who freely gave up vacation time to offer those skills for rebuilding efforts. These people had the know-how to complete the more intricate tasks; they were in great demand.

There were groups with members who had no clue where or how to begin. They wanted to do something and trusted that they would be told or taught what to do. Many times, the work they did allowed the more savvy skilled laborers to be more efficient.

Family members arrived together to offer their services. Sisters, brothers, fathers, sons, mothers, and daughters joined groups or made their own group and came. They reveled in the opportunity to spend this time with one another, giving of themselves.

Individuals showed up who were not parts of any group. They independently made their way to Mississippi with a desire to help. At the camp, they were welcomed and often "adopted" by teams comprised of people whom they had never before met.

Women and men who had suffered through their own tragedies moved past their personal grief to offer assistance. Their heavy hearts found solace in lifting the burden from another's heavy load. Many times, they became much-needed listeners to the sad stories.

In the coming week, they would wait in lines for the shower, surrendering the long hot showers to which they may have been accustomed so that everyone could have *some* hot water. They would patiently wait in lines again for food in the dining tent and eat what was offered. They would sleep on unfamiliar beds, trying to stay warm or cool, depending on the season. During free time in the evenings, they would entertain themselves in the only communal space available— the dining tent—by playing cards or board games or sharing stories in small groups or finding a spot to read or a place to make a phone call home.

Not only were all these volunteers giving of their time and skills, but they paid to give. They covered their own travel expenses. They gave a donation to the camp to cover the cost of the food and utilities. Many offered funds to the recovery organization to defray the cost of materials and equipment or would help with a special financial need of a homeowner.

This giving, this self-sacrifice, was proffered with no expectation of anything in return. At the end of the week as tools and supplies were collected from the job site, the homeowners would stop by to extend their sincere gratitude and to marvel at what had been accomplished. Enthusiastic hugs were exchanged in spite of dirty clothes and hands from the day's efforts. The group would assemble around the family for a picture, faces smiling with tears streaming down cheeks. Volunteers and homeowners alike would be overwhelmed with emotion at the gift that had been given to this family who had been strangers only a few days prior, but were now considered friends.

Emotions also ran high back at camp as bags were packed; addresses, emails and phone numbers were exchanged; and good-byes were conveyed. This shared experience of giving created a lasting bond; not just among those who traveled together, but with all those who participated in the events of the week. No one would be the same. This encounter deeply filled the soul of each and every person involved. Each and every person would declare, "I received much more than I gave."

Coming and Going (and Coming and Going)

Why do volunteers keep returning? Why have some come back six or seven times? Why have some sold their home in another state and moved to the Gulf Coast? What draws them?

Is it because the need is so great? There are homes that have not yet been touched. Vacant homes with boarded windows and blue tarps still dot the streets. Huge roll off dumpsters sporadically sit in front of houses where deconstruction and reconstruction are taking place.

Is it because one has the ability to help? All the skills learned in a lifetime come to fruition in this effort. The expertise acquired in training for a job, in volunteering to help a friend, in maintaining and remodeling one's own home all come together. The techniques gleaned from hours of watching home improvement shows add to the mix. All those experiences come together in one place at one time.

Is it a sense of achievement in a job well done or new skills learned? Those who know how to do things like hanging drywall and mudding, or cutting trim and nailing it in place, or installing a sink, or hanging siding, or just hammering a nail are willing to teach others. In sharing knowledge, confidence grows. Those who learn new skills gain a sense of achievement at accomplishing some new undertaking. It's energizing.

Is it the gratitude that is constantly expressed? Everyone has a need to be appreciated. The people of the Gulf Coast certainly do not hesitate to express their thanks. Just standing in line at a checkout counter, a volunteer is recognized as being a stranger in the area and thanked. Thanks are offered whether you have done something for that person directly or not.

Is it the graciousness and welcoming spirit of the people who live on the coast? Passersby deliver waves of "hellos." An invitation to sit and talk for a spell is extended. A smile of congeniality is flashed when strolling through the grocery store. A question about your well-being is asked by the waitress as you eat a meal. All these things combine in an expression of "I'm glad to know you. You matter to me."

Is it a heart of compassion that weeps at the loss? The loss is tremendous. It is not just loss of house, but also loss of home. It is loss of loved ones and neighbors and families moved on. It is loss of memories in pictures and mementos, trophies and ribbons, toys and keepsakes and of all the trappings that demonstrate a life lived. Gone. Washed away or ruined. Grieving is more bearable if someone will listen and share the burden. Every telling of the story lifts a layer of accumulated sorrow. The yearning of a heart filled with compassion finds a place here.

Is it simply a servant's heart compelled to help? There is a pull that draws one in. It is a knowing that a difference can be made. In returning again and again, that difference becomes more obvious. There is purpose here. Something concrete and visible can be done to illustrate the desire to help when words are not sufficient.

Is it relief that the disaster did not strike their home? The destruction was so total. What did remain was soaked, and molded and rotted. Where do you start with a mess like that?

Mixed emotions arise. There is sadness for the devastation, but gratitude that one's own home stands intact.

Is it because God has called? It is the quiet inner voice that says, "That's your job. I created you to do this." It is kind of like an itch that can only be scratched by going. In coming and building, the restlessness ceases, and the heart is filled.

Whatever the reason for coming, people of the Gulf Coast are eternally grateful. The words, "If it weren't for the volunteers, we'd have nothing," are repeated over and over again. The seemingly slow rebuilding is steadily moving forward. Life is returning. It is a different life. Much has changed. Much has been learned. There is hope.

Third Voice Faith Reflections

As the Gulf Coast was rebuilt, so were lives enhanced, changed or resurrected. Those who came to help were surprised at what they received in return. Some acquired new skills learned at the hand of other volunteers. These skills returned home with them to continue to be used personally or for volunteer opportunities locally. Some were filled with new confidence and purpose in living each day. All were filled with a soul-gratifying knowledge that they had made a difference.

God also provided lessons to be learned. Some learned of humility. Serving requires meeting the needs of those you serve rather than personal expectations. Sometimes volunteers arrived with a preconceived agenda about how much they would accomplish in a week. What they did not understand was that there were times that the most important need was to listen to a homeowner's story. Taking the time to listen offered a healing balm to a wounded heart that a house of wood and metal could not provide.

Another lesson helped some to understand that all work offered with a heart of love for our fellow man has importance, no matter how small or menial the task. Sanding porch railings to be reused or stair steps to be polished, cleaning windows and sweeping away the day's dirt were valued and necessary jobs.

Some learned of patience. There are times when high energy is necessary and things move along quickly. There are times when a slow, meandering pace is best. A gentler pace gives time for the joy of the moment and appreciation of others. It allows caring connections to form. God is more easily heard in quiet times.

Others learned things about themselves that they never knew before—untapped skills, a willingness to learn, and a capacity to care very deeply for folks they had never known, but who now are so often present in their minds and hearts. These new learnings kept many

187

volunteers coming back again and again, for more discoveries, and even in their mildly determined ways, to claim ownership of the progress being made. They wanted to keep coming back until the work was done.

What is the driving force behind the hundreds of volunteers who often use vacation time from work to travel long distances at their own expense, only to rise early and work long, hard days, and return to camp bone tired and smelly dirty? It is their faith. It is faith that God has called them to this task, that it is the right thing to do. It is faith that God will use their imperfections to accomplish His work. It is faith that they only need an eager spirit and compassionate heart. These faithful know that God will use whoever is willing and that those who are willing are blessed in return.

Fourth Voice:

Stories of Faith—
Written and Unwritten,
Lived Out and Hoped For

Psalm 51 (from the *New Revised Standard Version*)
Prayer for Cleansing and Pardon
To the leader: A Psalm of David, when the prophet Nathan
came to him, after he had gone into Bathsheba

Have mercy on me, O God, according to your steadfast love;
according to your abundant mercy blot out my
transgressions.
Wash me thoroughly from my iniquity, and cleanse me from
my sin.
For I know my transgressions and my sin is ever before me.
Against you, you alone have I sinned, and done what is evil in
your sight, so that you are justified in your sentence and
blameless when you pass judgment.
Indeed I was born guilty, a sinner when my mother conceived
me.
You desire truth in the inward being; therefore teach me
wisdom in my secret heart.
Purge me with hyssop, and I shall be clean; wash me and I
shall be whiter than snow.
Let me hear joy and gladness; let the bones that you crushed
rejoice.
Hide your face from my sins, and blot out all my iniquities.
Create in me a clean heart, O God, and put a new and right
spirit within me.
Do not cast me away from your presence, and do not take
your holy spirit from me.
Restore to me the joy of your salvation, and sustain in me a
willing spirit.
Then I will teach transgressors your ways, and sinners will
return to you.

Deliver me from bloodshed, O God, O God of my salvation,
and my tongue will sing aloud of your deliverance.

O Lord, open my lips and my mouth will declare your praise.

For you have no delight in sacrifice; if I were to give a burnt
offering, you would not be pleased.

The sacrifice acceptable to God is a broken spirit; a broken
and contrite heart, O God you will not despise.

Do good to Zion in your good pleasure; rebuild the walls of
Jerusalem,

then you will delight in right sacrifices, in burnt offerings and
whole burnt offering; then bulls will be offered on your
altar.[6]

As we listened to the voices speaking about Hurricane Katrina, we heard in each voice an underlying voice supporting and informing their stories. This is the voice of God at work creating, renewing, restoring, and upholding people of faith in their times of greatest need.

This chapter listens to the voice of God through the biblical witness. Psalm 51, holding within its verses God's acts of creating, renewing, restoring, and upholding, is chosen as a primary text for consideration, with New Testament stories from the life of Jesus and the teachings of Paul also included as they remind of us God's ever-present help and aid.

To entitle this treatment as the "fourth voice" is a misnomer, at least in part; God's voice is the primary voice as well as the ultimate voice in our lives and world. Yet, we listen to the fourth voice now as we explicitly enfold these stories in the language they have already spoken implicitly, the language of faith.

Informing Life and Faith—Psalm 51

In his thoughtful treatment, *With A Listening Heart: Biblical and Spiritual Reflections on the Psalms*, Bertrand Buby identifies Psalm 51 as the most moving of the seven psalms known as the "Penitential Psalms," describing its contents as "such an honest confession of sin that both in the synagogue and the church this psalm touches the heart of those praying it."[7] Psalms categorized as penitential give voice to the oft-silent nature of human remorse and express the need to be forgiven. A penitential psalm, such as Psalm 51, recognizes human sinfulness and cries out for the forgiveness that only God can give.

Psalm 51 greets and even accosts Christian worshippers every year at the beginning of the church's most penitential season—the season of Lent. On Ash Wednesday, Psalm 51 provides the framework upon which the honest and heartfelt desires of Christians are hung.

First, the Psalm recognizes and names the transgressions of one of Israel's most famous sinners—David. The superscription, which is an introduction to the Psalm, which notes the author of the Psalm, and the circumstances for which it is written, connects the Psalm most directly to David's adulterous affair with Bathsheba. This superscription is most likely a later addition, as the verses that follow are general in nature, and make note of historical references at the end of the Psalm, which link it to a much later historical event. It is doubtful, then, that there is a simultaneous correlation between the words of the Psalm and the superscription that introduces it. Even so, the Psalm describes sinfulness in such a way that it could describe David's remorse for his sin, or the remorse that any one of us feels when our sinfulness is great.

Second, the Psalm speaks of the most powerful ways that God's mercy can overcome human sinfulness. Verses 10-12 are key:

"Create in me a clean heart, O God, and put a new and
    right spirit within me.

Do not cast me away from your presence, and do not
    take your holy spirit from me.

Restore to me the joy of your salvation, and sustain in me
    a willing spirit."

A worshipful reading of the psalm progresses from reality of sinfulness to realization of hopefulness. The psalm guides the reader through the recognition of what he/she has failed to do, to more poignantly identify what God can and does do. The classic Christian (Protestant) tension—"The Law convicts, the Gospel saves"—weaves its way through regrets of the past (the law convicts) and into hopes for the future (the Gospel saves).

The request for God's action and activity in verses 10 through 12—"create," "put," "do not cast," "do not take," "restore," "sustain"—are powerful and speak of timely, even as it is timeless, activity on behalf of God's beloved creation. God reaches back to the beginning of time, and reaches forward to the fulfillment of all things, in order to make us whole.

The stories shared in First, Second, and Third Voices are, at their core, stories of faith, a faith informed by the living witness of the word of God. What God has done throughout the witness of Scripture God continues to do; thus, the Bible is a living word, not a historical document. For as many stories shared above, there are numerous Bible verses, stories, and references, which have woven their way into the stories of what faith looks like and feels like in the eye of the storm.

We use Psalm 51 as our starting point in reflecting on these stories of faith as its language and concepts, in just a few short verses, draw us very deeply into the hope of what God can do. In creating, renewing, restoring, and upholding as only God can do, we know of our reliance upon the strength of God, even and especially in the most difficult of circumstances. Those who have their own stories about Katrina to share have experienced and continue to experience how God was and is at work in all things.

Creating

"Create in me, a clean heart, O God…" those who pray these words of Psalm 51:10 call to mind God's ability to create out of nothing (Genesis 1:1) and God's continual work in creation. Creation of anything and everything by human hands finds its origin in the creative work of God. Humans are situated within God's creation, experiencing its beauty and its power. We view a sunset, and we marvel. We watch a flower grow and bloom, and we delight. We experience the birth of a child, and we rejoice.

We experience a natural disaster, and we tremble. Reminiscent of the pre-creation chaos, we experience the unguarded force of nature. Those who experienced Katrina learned firsthand of the power of the mighty wind and rushing sea; they learned firsthand of the volatility of human structures and the frailty of human life. Those who served in the aftermath saw the destructive effects of the storm, as they cleaned up and helped to rebuild.

A story of Jesus in the gospel of Mark (4:35-41) and its parallel passages (Matthew 8:23-27; Luke 8:22-25) tells of the power of a storm as it also tells of the superior power of Jesus. In the darkness and still of the night, Jesus and his disciples are traveling across the sea when a storm rocks their boat and shakes their faith. Awakened by the disciples' panic and fear, Jesus stills the storm, and inspires their awe (Mark 4:41) and marvel (Matthew 8:27; Luke 8:25). "Who then is this, that even wind and sea obey him?" (Mark 4:41)

Christians have also understood this story to speak powerfully to the metaphorical storms of life. A prayer from the *Lutheran Book of Worship* puts it this way: "O God, our defender, storms rage about us and cause us to be afraid. Rescue your people from despair; deliver your sons and daughters from fear, and preserve us all from unbelief, through your Son, Jesus Christ our Lord."[8] And, a familiar hymn prays this prayer: "O Savior, whose almighty word, the winds and waves submissive heard, who walked upon the foaming deep and calm amid the storm didst sleep: Oh hear us when we cry to thee for those in peril on the sea" ("Eternal Father, Strong to Save").[9]

Not all of life's storms are comprised of wind and water, lightening rod and quake; not all of life's storms damage or destroy only what is physical. In fact, most of life's storms strike from within, unsettling and upending our minds, our hearts, and our souls—shaking the very core of our being.

"Create in me a clean heart, O God…" In the language of the Old Testament, the only subject of the verb "to create" is God; to create is to "bring into existence what was not there before."[10] And in understanding the Hebrew concept of "heart," there is the recognition that the heart is the seat of human intellect and guides human decision-making. For God to create a new heart is to bring newness into the very core of the human being. For God to create a new heart is for God to create something which previously did not exist.

Looking beyond the wreckage and the rubble, and looking behind the bricks and the mortar, stories of faith in the eye of the storm bring this notion of God's creation to light time and time again. God's creative hand is at work in reforming the hearts of his people. Having experienced the force of the chaos, faithful people are now living into the power of what is new and vital and essential. Faithful people are now recognizing, like never before, how God creates, out of the nothingness, the fullness of all things. *The Message,* a popular paraphrase of the Bible into modern thought and language, puts it this way: "God, make a fresh start in me, shape a Genesis week from the chaos of my life."[11]

God's creative force forms the chaos into something new, which is more powerful than anything of human design.

Renewing

"…and put a new and right spirit within me." The psalmist's plea continues for that which is new, as opposed to the cleansing of that which is former, or old. Renewal is synonymous with creation, as is heart with spirit. That is to say, God is making both heart and spirit in God's newness, and that heart and spirit are where the self is expressed as they "characterize the condition and direction of a person's life."[12]

Verse 10 points to a marked difference in thought and tone, moving away from the language of forgiveness and cleansing in the previous verses 1-9 and into the language of newness. A clean heart and a new and right spirit speak of the stability and steadfastness that come from within.[13] There is recognition that behind outward sinfulness are the inner motives of heart and spirit that can only be remedied by God's working to radically change the core of a human being. Arthur Weiser puts it this way: "…and when man is to overcome his own self, he cannot do so by virtue of his own efforts, but only with the help of steadfast spirit given to him by God."[14]

The adjective translated as "right" in the New Revised Standard Version of the Bible can and has also been translated as "steadfast." The Hebrew word denotes the sense of something which is firm and solid and in the context of this Psalm contrasts external facades of stability with true inward stability of the spirit. A steadfast spirit, a spirit renewed by God, is ready to praise God, to remain true to God's promises, and to trust God in times of trouble.[15]

The psalmist returns to these central notions of heart and spirit in verse 17: "The sacrifice acceptable to God is a broken spirit; a broken and contrite heart, O God, you will not despise." God's creating and renewing continues every time our human nature corrupts what is our divine nature. Offering our brokenness to God is our admission that we cannot rely on our own merits, but in humility, we offer ourselves back to God so that God's work can begin anew. A simple praise song, "Change my heart, O God," reflects back and forward to the divine image, ever created and renewed in the human image: "Change my heart, O God, make it ever new. Change my heart, O God, may I be like You."[16]

In the United States Gulf Coast, following Hurricane Katrina, signs of renewal are at first outwardly obvious. Inconceivable amounts of physical devastation have been hauled off and moved out, making way for property, landscape and seascape, which is fresh and new. Treasures ravaged by the storm and turned into rubble have been collected and redesigned into creative remembrances, and destroyed trees have been renewed into works of art. Damaged homes have been replaced by newer and even stronger dwellings; countless blue roof tarps have made way to new roofs, more sound and reliable than the ones they replaced.

Beyond the visible and outward renewal, Gulf Coast dwellers and visitors can pause and sense the inner renewal of the spirit and heart. Stories of heroism during the storm recall a demonstration of strength beyond physical realities which relied on the inward strength of heart and spirit. Stories of clean-up, call to mind the outpouring of the efforts of early responders who jumped into the messiness with a heart and spirit of service. Stories of rebuilding celebrate, in the midst of countless hours of hammering, sawing, and painting, the timeless moments of lives being renewed in heart and in spirit.

In his letter to the Romans, Paul addresses the new Christian community in Rome using the language of renewal: "Do not be conformed to this world, but be transformed by the renewing of your minds, so that you may discern what the will of God—what is good and acceptable and perfect"

(Romans 12:2). What is renewed by God in heart and spirit is active in the renewal of the mind, so that discernment of the will of God, as opposed to human will, is possible.

Paul goes on to encourage his readers to use this discernment for the benefit of the entire body of Christ. Discernment of the renewed mind within the body of Christ serves to remind all Christians of their humility, before God and in service to others. Discerning minds recognize that no one is fully equipped on his or her own to serve all the needs of the people of God. Each person is uniquely gifted, one from another, for service in Christ's name.

Renewal of heart, mind, and spirit is the work of God for which we sincerely pray; we continually seek to express our openness to the ways in which God will renew us and change us. Renewal in the context of community recognizes our mutual need to be changed and forever changing in Christ. Renewal in community does not happen simultaneously to all members of the body, but is happening continually, flowing in and through each of the parts of the body for its upbuilding and strength.

This dynamic nature of renewal has been a remarkable occurrence within the lives of those affected by Hurricane Katrina. Survivors of the storm have been renewed by the witness of those who have come to their aid. Relief workers and volunteers have been renewed by the witness of survivors who braved the storm and who refuse to give up. Hearts and spirits, made new by God, are shared. Lives, which praise God, remain true to God's promises. Souls, which trust God in times of trouble, are re-equipped.

Restoring

"Restore to me the joy of your salvation…" In verse 12, the psalmist prays for the restoration of joy. The joy of God's salvation, ever-present, is often obscured by the changes and chances of life. In newness of heart and spirit, God lifts the veil of our circumstances so that we can see and feel that joy again. It is often in the remembrance of our joy of the past and in anticipation that we will experience God's joy again, that we are sustained in life's most difficult of circumstances. According to Weiser's interpretation, "joy in the helpful nearness of God" is "the actual motive-power of the new way of life."[17]

On his way to the cross, and in gathering his disciples together for one last meal, Jesus speaks of the joy that his disciples will know and share: "I have said these things to you so that my joy may be in you, and that your joy may be complete" (John 15: 11). This reminder of Christ's joy comes to heart-heavy disciples, anticipating the dreadful events of the next few days. This reminder of Christ's joy is also couched between Jesus' two commandments to his disciples to love: to abide in Jesus' love, just as he abides in his Father's love (15:9) and to love one another, just as Jesus has demonstrated his sacrificial love to them (15:12-13).

For Jesus, to live into the joy of God's salvation is to live lives of love, toward God and toward one another. Jesus also teaches his disciples that the tasks of love entrusted to them will not be solely their own endeavors—that the Advocate, the Holy Spirit, will assist them and will guide them in their love and service to God and to one another (John 14:15-17, 25-26; 15:26-27; 16:7-11).

In Psalm 51:11, there is one of two Old Testament references to the Holy Spirit (see also Isaiah 63:10-11); the Holy Spirit has "the enlivening effect of God's work on the psalmist."[18] A clean heart and a new and right spirit are enlivened by the Holy Spirit so that God's joy may be known and lived within the life of faith.

"Lord, make us instruments of your peace. Where there is hatred, let us sow love; where there is injury, pardon; where there is discord, union; where there is doubt, faith; where there is despair, hope; where there is darkness, light; *where there is sadness, joy*" (prayer attributed to St. Francis—emphasis mine).

We have discussed above how creation and renewal are evident in the lives of those affected by Hurricane Katrina. Identifying moments of the restoration of joy bid recognition of God's work at a new level. Restoration of joy asks for recognition of clean hearts and new and right spirits in the tasks of every day and ongoing life. Restoration of joy asks for recognition in relationship with God and of one another.

Even the most courageous, most hopeful, and most profound stories of faith in the eye of the storm wonder out loud as to whether or not there will be joy again. Will my life ever be the same after the storm? What happens the "next time"? Will I ever be able to live without fear and in joy again?

Katrina survivors and those who face all types of the storms of life have come to realize that the life of faith is not a guarantee that daily living will be easy or non-challenging— "Storms rage around us and cause us to be afraid" (see p.198 above, a prayer from *Lutheran Book of Worship*). The guarantee is not in a carefree life, but in a life in which we are cared for—deeply—by God. Life offers a storm, God offers salvation, and we live in the joy of knowing and sharing that God is with us. Living in joy is living in between the storms of life, and celebrating that salvation is a gift from God that cannot be drenched by the torrent and downpour of life.

Restoring our joy is also in the living of lives of love. Faith responding in the eye of the storm has produced countless stories of people sharing their love with others, most often not even knowing those with whom they have been called into a relationship of love. It is a relationship of love that rejoices in what is good and positive and suffers together through what is bad and negative. It is a relationship of love that binds hearts and hands together for a common purpose and a common good. It is a relationship of love that leaves and takes pieces of servants' hearts to and from sandy shores and rehabbed rooftops and binds them together and into the heart of Christ.

Upholding

"...and sustain in me a willing spirit."

Even in recognizing that in all of life, God is continually at work making things new, the psalmist hopes and prays that God's created goodness will be sustained. The psalmist wants to experience God's joy and to be right with God once more. In praying to be sustained (the Revised Standard Version reads, "and uphold me with a willing spirit"), the psalmist's heartfelt request is to remain in right relationship with God.

Anyone who prays in this way inevitably knows how life gets in the way, and draws us away from the new possibilities God creates in us. We fail, we grow tired, and we put ourselves above God and above others. During these moments in life, we especially recognize our need to be sustained and upheld by God.

During his public ministry, Jesus demonstrated a profound sensitivity to the cares and the needs of the people he encountered. As he taught them, he knew that they were looking for answers to the questions of their faith. As he healed them, he knew the weight of the illnesses and diseases that burdened them. As he lived among them, he knew of the particular needs of the poor and the outcast—those most disregarded by the society in which they lived.

In Matthew 11, following a time of teaching with his disciples and a time of prayer to his Father, Jesus extends this invitation: "Come to me, all you that are weary and are carrying heavy burdens, and I will give you rest. Take my yoke upon you, and learn from me; for I am gentle and humble in heart, and you will find rest for your souls. For my yoke is easy, and my burden is light" (Matthew 11:28-30).

In these words, Jesus extends the most gracious and generous of invitations to the most wearied hearts and souls. We know that during our times of greatest need, we do not carry our burdens alone. We know that the one whose death and resurrection carries us into eternal life also carries us throughout all our lives.

There has been a remarkable awareness among those affected by Hurricane Katrina that God has been and continues to be the one who upholds us in all things. The burden of the storm has been great and for many simply too much to bear, at least too much to bear alone. Realizing that God is at work upholding his people has given to many the strength to make it through these most difficult of circumstances.

Also, the burden of the storm has been shared among survivors, relief workers, and volunteers. The burden of rebuilding has been shared and the load has been lightened. The burden of the emotional trauma caused by the storm has been shared through its retelling and listening, and the load has been lightened. The financial burden caused by the storm has been shared through generous giving, and the load has been lightened.

On the last day of my most recent trip to the Gulf Coast, I stopped by a home that was being rebuilt by disaster response staff and volunteers. "You're just in time," were the words that greeted me in the doorway. "We're ready to install the new countertop." And so we did, one supervisor from the staff and six volunteers—from Pennsylvania, Iowa and Michigan—took our places, maneuvered our way from the dining room to an inside kitchen wall, where we carefully placed the new countertop where it belonged. It was heavy, and designed carefully for a particular space, so we had to work together to install it just right.

Sharing in the enormity of the task of rebuilding following Hurricane Katrina has been a demonstration, time and time again, of how people of faith are upholding other people of faith. Only because God upholds us can we uphold one another. Only because Christ carries our burdens are we strengthened to carry the burdens of one another.

"Grant that we may not so much seek to be consoled as to console; to be understood as to understand; to be loved as to love. For it is in giving that we receive; it is in pardoning that we are pardoned; and it is in dying that we are born to eternal life" (prayer attributed to St. Francis).

The Fourth Voice

As the subtitle of the book (*Katrina Stories in Four Voices*) promises, we have listened to the fourth and final voice—the voice of God speaking through God's Word. We have heard and discovered what each voice brings to these stories of faith. God's voice has been informing each of the other voices and the stories told. God's Word has bound these stories of faith with stories of faith written and unwritten, lived out and hoped for. As people continue to experience profound losses and challenges, God's voice will sustain them with the assurance that God speaks words of comfort and hope, even in the eye of the storm.

Fourth Voice Faith Reflections

Think of a time in your life when you experienced a great challenge or hardship. Was there a verse, chapter, or story from Scripture that spoke to you? Or, during a time of great joy, did you call to mind a song of praise from the Bible?

As you continue to read and reflect on God's word, look for verses and chapters that you might commit to memory and take to heart. Who knows how and when they will inform and strengthen you in your hour of need?

Lasting Voices:

Stories of Faith—
Past, Present, Future

Looking Back

He had no choice. That is, unless he wanted to give up everything he knew. Give up his home, his family, his job, his country. Drafted. First, he endured basic training and jump school, followed by Special Forces training. Next came fourteen months in Vietnam as a Green Beret, spending forty days in the field at a time running ground surveillance radar. The days stretched as he labored through the final hours "in country." However, surviving and coming home meant more tough times.

At the airport in Chicago, he was spit upon and called a "baby killer." After he met his little son for the first time, his wife of less than two years announced that she wanted a divorce. How do you handle that? What do you do with the memories of losing a buddy, witnessing the explosion that takes off half his face? How do you reconcile the death of your "adopted" ten-year-old Vietnamese son because he picked up a land mine? He suppressed it, stuffed it, and tried to forget about it.

Life went on. Years passed. Memories rarely surfaced anymore. He came to Biloxi, Mississippi, to help rebuild homes. It was during his fourth trip to Biloxi that some things changed.

February was a slow month for volunteers. This particular week only saw ten new arrivals in Camp Biloxi. After dinner each night, the small group would linger in the huge dining tent and share stories. One evening, Barry mentioned that he had served in Vietnam. Dale remarked that he had also served.

Dale got up from his seat at one table and moved to sit directly across from Barry at another table. As they matched dates and places, they realized that they both had operated from the same fire support base, Hill 411. Their conversation became animated as they identified more and more landmarks with which they were both familiar.

Then, Barry's voice became mellow. He shared stories that his second wife of thirty-five years had never before heard him tell. Slowly, others in the dining tent ceased their conversations and turned their solemn attention to Barry's words. Tears began to run down his cheeks and his voice cracked. Barry then received from his fellow volunteers in that big white, circus-like tent, with the plywood floor and plastic table and chairs, what he had needed—understanding and acceptance. Their voices echoed compassion and sympathy for all that he had endured.

Years of quashing emotions from those hard times had come to an end. Here in this storm-torn region his personal storms found solace. Katrina had brought these volunteers to this place. God had caused the right paths to cross to bring healing.

Looking Forward

Inherent in the task of parenting is wanting what is best for our children. We want to provide them with a safe and happy home; we want them to have the best education and learning experiences possible. And we hope to ground them in what we believe.

Mark was nearly fourteen years old when Hurricane Katrina landed on the United States Gulf Coast in 2005. In many ways, he was a typical middle school student who liked to hang out and play video games. He was quiet around people he did not know, and was not one to put himself forward as a leader or as a volunteer.

Like many young people his age, he would hear about the current event simply called Katrina, see countless visual images, and hear many stories of the effects of the storm. And, after many week-long absences of either of his parents, who were both traveling a couple of times a year as post-Katrina volunteers, Mark was intrigued enough and inquired about joining one of the mission trips. He accompanied a church group in 2008 and again in 2009. He got to see for himself the area he had learned about in school. He worked alongside others in the rebuilding effort. He met Gulf Coast residents and heard their stories of surviving the storm and rebuilding their lives. Most importantly, he came to the realization that the small part he played in the rebuilding efforts made a difference.

Leah was nine years old at the time of Katrina. In her young life, she had already been involved in helping others. She began raising money for the local Habitat for Humanity chapter when she was five years old, and was waiting impatiently for the time when she would be allowed, around the age of thirteen, to volunteer on the Habitat sites by passing out tools to the workers. Her expressed desire to travel to the Gulf Coast preceded her parents' trips to the region. Her first trip to Mississippi would be in 2010; she would be part of the rebuilding efforts, and would also see and experience the winding down of some of the volunteer camps there.

A unique experience Leah would have was to accompany her mother to two interviews conducted for this book. Her interest in doing so was great, and she took detailed notes of these interviews. It was apparent that Leah listened intensely and intently as one Biloxi resident and one young woman, who came to Mississippi as an early long-term volunteer, told their stories. Leah continues to refer back to these interviews as having a profound impact on her life and even keeps in touch with those who were interviewed that day.

For Mark and Leah, their world changed and was profoundly marked by the horrific events of September 11, 2001, and continues to be marked by our nation's involvement in military conflict across the world, by economic hardship, and by natural disasters. In their young lives, they have seen the worst; consequently, they have also seen the best. They have seen bravery and valor in young men and women not much older than themselves. They have seen volunteerism and community service that has made a difference. They have seen the self-determination of those who have struggled, but have worked very hard, to turn their lives around.

And, Mark and Leah have been part of the solution. With their own personalities and unique gifts, they have helped. They have joined their classmates, friends, and other young church members in unprecedented volunteer and community service efforts. In an era where community service and volunteer projects are even a part of academic curricula, our young people are learning that they can make a difference.

Building on their Katrina experiences, Mark and Leah show a continued interest in devoting their lives to serving others. From a parent's perspective, having my children involved in disaster relief work was the best possible learning, character building, and faith-informing activity I could have hoped for them. May the witness and enthusiastic commitment of our youth give us hope for a world that will not be free of tragedy and pain, but will be full of hands and hearts willing to serve.

May It Be So

Poet Cee Cee Jay Spencer begins her poem "The Last Word" with these thoughts: "As I hold this pen and the letters are formed on this paper, one more time I've silenced my voice. Sitting back resting now wondering if nature will take its course, as the old people used to say…"

A return to silence. Not the silence of the original devastation where there was no sound—not of bird, insect, or mechanical hum—buts the silence at the day's end when long hours of exertion pause. It is the silence of wondering what tomorrow will bring. It is the silence that settles as sleep overtakes us. It is the silence of turning it all over to the God of comfort with confidence that He will provide.

This silence is one of expectation and hope. It is trusting, believing, knowing that God is present in the middle of it all. He is there in the storm, in the aftermath, in the rebuilding.

The poet sums it up this way: "The creator will always have the last word. The creator will always have the last word." Trusting in the splendor of creation and the goodness of the Creator, may it be so!

Endnotes

[1] Lutheran Disaster Response (LDR) is a collaborative ministry of the Evangelical Lutheran Church in America (ELCA) and The Lutheran Church—Missouri Synod (LCMS). LDR seeks to demonstrate Christ's compassion for all people by promoting hope, healing, and wholeness for disaster survivors. LDR initially helped to establish Camp Biloxi, a place for volunteers to stay while assisting in recovery work following Hurricane Katrina. For more information or to volunteer, go to: http://www.ldr.org/

[2] Recovery Assistance, Inc. Ministries (RAI Ministries) restores faith, home, and community in the Name of Jesus Christ. In September 2007, RAI Ministries assumed operation of the volunteer hospitality operations of Camp Biloxi and assumed full operation of the camp from April 2008 until Aug. 29, 2010. In addition, RAI operates Camp Restore, a volunteer camp in New Orleans, Louisiana. Volunteer groups and staff physically rebuild family dwellings, churches, and schools and participate in numerous community projects while providing emotional and spiritual care to those in need. For more information or to volunteer, go to: http://www.raiministries.org/

[3] These introductory pages are indebted to three persons who were interviewed and shared their stories and perspectives. Donna Tasker is a Biloxi resident who was integral in the early stages of storm recovery in assisting with volunteer coordination at Bethel Lutheran Church in Biloxi, a partner in the efforts of Lutheran Disaster Response. Donna continues to share her gifts for helping with the recovery as part of the staff of the Bethel Free Health Clinic in Biloxi. Allison Rollison was an early volunteer in Biloxi whose gifts for social work and case management proved extremely helpful in the initial as well as the long-term recovery. Though not a native, Allison now resides in the area and continues to be an asset to the social needs of residents in the area. Tim Brown, a Pennsylvania resident, was called upon early to set up housing for the volunteers who would come to help. Tim, representing Lower Susquehanna Lutheran Disaster Response, led the efforts to construct a "Tent City" on the grounds of Good Shepherd Lutheran Church in Biloxi, which came to be known as Camp

Biloxi. Tim, and spouse Rosanne, worked side by side and fought some of the early battles of securing the necessary funding and materials to support and sustain the volunteer relief effort. As these introductory pages were written, the observations and insights of Donna, Allison, and Tim flowed together in such a way that to attribute each comment to one of them seemed intrusive. The authors are most grateful for their contributions to the recovery efforts and for what they have shared with us.

[4] Cee Cee Jay Spencer on writing "Katrina: Poetry in Two Distinct Voices" has this to say: "The initial purpose for writing the poetry book was to help with my own healing after living through the Katrina experience. But as I was writing the book, I also felt that if it happened to come into the hands of other families who have had this experience, or similar experiences like people who may have gone through the tsunamis or the California wildfires, or any type of natural disaster, it could help them as well. I was thinking that as they try to come together and get a sense of some normalcy that they could read this together with parents, with grandparents, with aunts, with uncles or other family members who may have had this particular experience. The poems are written in two voices so that two people can read it together. It could be a mother and a child. It could be a grandmother or a grandfather and a child. It could be an aunt and a child. Or, it could be two adults, if the children are under the age of actually reading some of the words which are rather large. My mission and my thought for the book, is to have it translated into a couple different languages sometime in the future. My desire for the book is to go out and just be a blessing to as many people as possible, not only here in the United States, but all over the world."

[5] The Extra Mile Ministries Crisis Response Team is comprised of K9 Comfort Dogs, experienced handlers and team members. The dogs are a vital link in the ministry of national response to crisis/disaster. These specially trained comfort dogs work with experienced handlers and team members in stressful situations that are often chaotic and unpredictable. The team helps victims, emergency personal, and family members cope emotionally and spiritually. In doing so the team is able to help renew faith and

restore hope. Executive director, Chaplain Ralph Buchhorn. For more information, go to: http://www.faceofcrisis.org.

6 The translation used for Psalm 51 and other passages quoted form the Bible are from the New Revised Standard Version of *The New Oxford Annotated Bible*, ed. Bruce M. Metzger and Roland E. Murphy (Oxford University Press: New York) 1991.

7 Bertrand Buby, *With a Listening Heart: Biblical and Spiritual Reflections on the Psalms*, p. 57.

8 Prayer for the fifth Sunday after Pentecost, from *Lutheran Book of Worship*, (Augsburg Publishing House, Minneapolis and Board of Publication, Lutheran church in America: Philadelphia) 1978, p.25.

9 Also from *Lutheran Book of Worship*, Hymn number 467.

10 James Luther Mays, *Psalms [Interpretation: A Bible Commentary for Teaching and Preaching]*, p. 202.

11 *The Message* is a contemporary paraphrase of the Bible, by Eugene Peterson (NavPress: Colorado Springs) 2005.

12 Mays, p.2

13 Dennis Bratcher, "Psalm 51 and the Language of Transformation: A Biblical Perspective on Holiness", p. 6.

14 Arthur Weiser, *The Psalms* [Old Testament Library], p. 407.

15 Mays, p. 203.

16 "Change My Heart, O God", by Eddie Espinoza.

17 Weiser, p. 407.

18 Roland Murphy, *The Gift of the Psalms*, p. 99.

Bibliography

Bratcher, Dennis. "Psalm 51 and the Language of Transformation: A Biblical Perspective on Holiness", a paper presented to the Theology Symposium, Korea Nazarene University, Chonan, South Korea—May 22, 2001. (http://www.crivoice.org/psa51.html).

Buby, Bertrand. *With a Listening Heart: Biblical and Spiritual Reflections on the Psalms*, Alba House, 2005.

Center for Oral History and Cultural Heritage, The University of Southern Mississippi, *Hurricane Katrina Oral History Project*, Vol. 929, 2007. Reprinted with permission of the publishers.

Mays, James Luther. *Psalms* [*Interpretation: A Bible Commentary for Teaching and Preaching*] (Louisville: John Knox, 1994).

Murphy, Roland. *The Gift of the Psalms* (Peabody, MA: Hendrickson, 2000).

Spencer, Cee Cee Jay. *Katrina: Poetry in Two Distinct Voices,* (iUniverse, 2007).

Weiser, Arthur. *The Psalms* [Old Testament Library] (Philadelphia: Westminster Press, 1962).

About the Authors

Janyce Jorgensen serves as a pastor in a congregational setting and as a professor in an ecumenical setting. Her primary interest in ecclesial as well as academic settings is the study of Scripture and how it informs the life of faith. She has contributed to an ecumenical treatment of Scripture and has written various articles on mission and service, ecumenical relationships and preaching. Since Hurricane Katrina, she has devoted an extensive amount of time to mission and service experiences in the U.S. Gulf Coast and Mexico. She resides in Pennsylvania with her husband and children.

Deb Anderson taught in the public school system for thirty-three years, primarily in middle school, and loved every minute of it! Within her church, she is extensively involved in caring and listening ministries. She helps to plan and lead amazing, God inspired, retreats for women. She has spent weeks on the Gulf Coast assisting with rebuilding homes and listening to the hearts of people who reside there as well as to those who come there to serve. Deb and her husband live in Pennsylvania and have four grown children who have encouraged her to be a better listener.

www.ingramcontent.com/pod-product-compliance
Lightning Source LLC
Chambersburg PA
CBHW061354280526
45784CB00001B/248